We're Not All the Same

We're Not All the Same

Why Generalising about Politicians Is Damaging Our Democracy – a Local Councillor's View

Tracey Hill

Illustrations by Jeanne Lolness

Copyright © 2022 T.M. Parris
All rights reserved.
ISBN-13: 978-1-7392054-0-9

Preface		7
1.	Introduction: They're All the Same	11
2.	They're Out of Touch	23
3.	They Don't Keep their Promises	35
4.	They're Always Bickering	49
5.	They're Boring	61
6.	They Lie	71
7.	They Don't Answer the Question	83
8.	They Don't Listen	91
9.	They Have No Guts	103
10.	They Only Want to Line their Own Pockets	113
11.	They're Incompetent	131
12.	Nothing Ever Changes	141
13.	So What?	153
14.	Acknowledgements	162
15.	About the Author	164
16.	Endnotes	165

Preface

We're Not All the Same

You may have assumed, as I did when growing up, that we would always have democracy. The right to choose our leaders, and to demand transparency and accountability from them, was hard won, and others elsewhere in the world are still fighting for it. By now we ought to accept that democracy is not perfect and its outcomes will not be perfect either. And yet I have the feeling, shared by other commentators, that we are falling out of love with it.

Democracy is not inevitable. In an era when a powerful dictator invades a sovereign European nation, and a former president who refused to accept an election result and watched on TV while a mob of his supporters ransacked the US Capitol decides to stand for another term in office, it doesn't seem out of place to wonder whether we are saying a long slow goodbye to a form of government that hasn't actually been around that long and never took off at all in many parts of the world.

Democracy, for all its imperfections, grants citizens certain rights to influence the decisions that are made on their behalf. If it came to it, how many of us would fight to retain these rights? There seem to be plenty who are so disillusioned with the whole thing that they would welcome an alternative. A report published by UK Onward in September 2022 called *The Kids Aren't All Right*[i] reported that 61% of 18-34 year olds think that "having a strong leader who does not have to bother with Parliament or elections would be a good way of running this country". Almost half (46%) of them felt that the army should run the country, and over a quarter (26%) thought that democracy was a bad way of doing it. The same study showed that support for democracy is inversely proportional to age: only amongst those over 65 was net support for democracy over 80%.

Why do so many seem willing to dismiss Parliament and elections as merely some long-winded encumbrance? Negative views about politicians and a lack of faith in politics in general is surely behind this. For those of us who are quite keen to retain our democratic rights to choose and to influence, that means it's time for the overwhelmingly negative perceptions of politics and politicians to be challenged.

Politicians are essential in a democracy. It's through our elected representatives that we can have some say in what happens. They have been chosen by us, to do our bidding. But somehow it doesn't feel that way. Of course there are times, such as the recent political instability which has exacerbated a cost of living crisis, when the electorate rightly feels let down by the actions of the people they have put in power. But this disappointment often seems to extend to all politicians, not just those who are directly responsible.

We choose our politicians, and yet we hate them. Perhaps we hate them because we choose them, because we have been persuaded they ought to be able to do a lot more for us than they actually can. Perhaps we blame them for the fact that other voters think differently about things. One way or another, our views of politicians are – to put it mildly – not positive, and that is damaging not only our support for democracy but also our ability to participate effectively in it.

A great deal of generalising goes on when politicians are being discussed. They're all the same. They're all in it for themselves. They all lie. And so on. The results of this: low turnout at election time, amongst other things. What's the point in voting, if they're all useless? We're also seeing abuse of politicians and attacks, not only on social media but also, sadly, in real life, with the murders of Jo Cox and David Amess all too front-of-mind. While acts of violence against politicians are thankfully rare, negative sentiments are not. Why are these views so prevalent?

If people were right, and politicians were uniformly rubbish, didn't care, were entirely self-serving and never listened, the promise offered by democracy to furnish citizens with some influence over the course taken by their nation and their local area would be a false one. If this were true, there would be no point in defending democracy. We may as well have a strongman. But I don't think it is true.

My view is that democracy basically works. Not always brilliantly and certainly not always quickly, but it does serve to put the values and desires of the voting public at the heart of political decision-making. This view, I know, has certain implications. It suggests that if things don't work the way we think they should, politicians are not necessarily solely to blame. It also means that the negative political tropes, the easy phrases that roll off the tongue and are seen everywhere in the press and social media, are unfounded, or at least – and this is critical – they're not true of all politicians.

Some politicians are dreadful. This much is certainly true. But all of them? That's the part that doesn't make sense. Every time someone states that all politicians are the same, a little angel of democracy loses its wings. Democracy works when we can distinguish the good, effective, honest politicians from those who are less so. If we hold the view that all politicians are bad, ineffective and dishonest, we are no longer distinguishing good from bad. We are not making any distinction between a politician who diligently serves their constituents and is effective at getting things done, and one who doesn't.

High standards are good, and those who hold office should adhere to them. But if we don't recognise any difference between those who meet these standards and those who don't, we are not imposing high standards. We're talking down the whole system.

High expectations are good: they are an affirmation of a general public belief in the potency of politics to fix our social problems. But if those expectations are so high that no one at all can possibly meet them, what results is universal disappointment and disaffection, a constant unhappiness which brings, over time, a disengagement with politics altogether.

Criticism is good: it's a key sign of an open and transparent society where politicians are held to account for their actions. But if criticism is all we hear, no one is being held to account. In our public discourse, do we get a balanced view? Do we hear about the successes as well as the failures? If we don't, how are we supposed to evaluate the people involved, and the parties and policies they advocate?

If the debate is unremittingly negative, the result will be a perception that our governance is a disaster and that everything attempted by a democratically-led public body will result in chaos. Looking around at the society in which we live, I don't think that is the case. If there are governments in some parts of the globe who are genuinely awful at everything they attempt, I would wager that they're not democracies. However, the language around politics suggests that many here in the UK have become persuaded that nothing good ever comes from politicians, of whatever background, party, or level of government.

Politics has become a dirty word, a topic that puts the dampeners on any social conversation. We have become programmed to see the bad in everyone, the down side of every decision. Being positive about politicians often feels like a brave thing to do – it certainly puts you in the minority in a lot of social situations – but it shouldn't. The whole point of democracy is that it enables us to hold different opinions while still getting on with the business of organising ourselves as a society. We ought to be able to support a particular person, party, viewpoint or ideology, and oppose another. Instead, so much rhetoric is directed indiscriminately against everybody – against, therefore, the system in its entirety. As a result we are not dealing in reality, but in a version of the world in which politicians – all of them – are almost exclusively to blame for the general wrongness of everything. To some this is quite convenient, as it points the finger at a particular group. It's also a vision of the world in which it might make sense for a strongman to dispense with all the trappings of democracy and just get on with the job. This is why I think that these tropes about politicians are so dangerous, and it is why I have written this book.

I'm not arguing that politicians are never to blame. They certainly are, at times, but not all of them, and not exclusively. I do argue, though, that politicians over time have made things a lot more difficult for themselves by being too eager to tell people what they want to hear, allowing expectations to spiral upwards through overly broad criticism of each other, and generalising too broadly about their opponents. Having said that, politicians are sometimes expected to be on both sides of an argument at once, and get caught between responding to public opinion and sticking to their inbuilt ideology. In reality these things have to be balanced and some judgement is needed about when to do what. Sometimes politicians get it right and sometimes they don't, but in the court of public opinion it often seems that they are condemned whatever they do.

It isn't just about what politicians do. It's about who they are. An image of an elite aristocracy divorced from reality is easy to create but less easy to defend when talking about the hundreds of thousands of people who have ever served as elected representatives. Most political news reporting and discussion, it seems to me, is about half a dozen or so people, the Prime Minister and some members of the front bench, plus the main opposition leaders. Whatever they do – if it's bad – ripples out to everyone. MPs and councillors know that people appreciate their work and express gratitude. But those who have direct dealings with their elected representatives are unfortunately in a small minority. The good politicians, of whom there are many, will try and do something about this by reaching out to their constituents. But they are staggering under a burden of negativity, much of which is simply assumed from national headlines.

Many of the examples in this book come from the time I served as a councillor on Brighton and Hove City Council. Local politics can be very immediate: it's in particular places, with particular deliverables in the offing (or not) that push really comes to shove. I aim to give a flavour of what the job was really like and to present actual examples of difficult issues: what people said, what they wanted and what our real-life options were (one of which relates to goldfish, in case you start wondering – chapter eleven). I also include experiences as a rank-and-file campaigner for other Labour candidates, and as a citizen and observer of national politics. As a result, throughout this book my pronouns are a bit all over the place. Are politicians "they" or "we"? Are they talking to us, the electorate, or are we talking to them? Well, I'm both, in different parts of the book, depending on the context. It seemed impossible only to be one or the other, so I can only hope I've made myself clear enough.

This book contains recollections going back as far as 2015 or even earlier. Conversations are approximate and I'm certainly not trying to embarrass any individuals; I rarely use names, and what is included here are examples of sentiments that were also expressed by others. I am a Labour Party member and supporter, but this book isn't intended to be party political: it's about the generalisations that people make across the entire political spectrum, although I'm sure my opinions will show through.

Plenty of people have served for longer than me or have greater expertise about what I'm discussing here. As I didn't want to speak for anyone else, at times the book seems to read as though I was out there by myself, and it was never like that. But these are definitely my views, and my views alone.

Not everyone is going to agree with the points I make in this book, but I hope you find it a useful contribution to the urgently-needed debate on political engagement. Feel free to comment on the Facebook page (search for *We're Not All the Same*) or contact me by some other means. As we say in all those leaflets, I'd love to hear from you!

Tracey Hill
Facebook: facebook.com/traceyhillprofile
Twitter: @TraceyMHill
Website: www.traceyhillauthor.co.uk

We're Not All the Same

Tracey Hill

1. Introduction: They're All the Same

Politicians, eh? What do they do? Nothing. They're stupid and they lie. They're out of touch, gutless, only in it for themselves. You can never get a straight answer out of them. They're corrupt, they spend all their time bickering, and they never, ever, listen.

I'm not here to defend the entire political establishment. Some of the above is certainly true of some politicians. And when it is true it needs to be exposed. The problem I have is the broad acceptance, whether it's implicit or stated, that this is true of *all* politicians – every single one of them.

I was a politician. I was elected onto Brighton and Hove City Council in May 2015, representing the ward of Hollingdean and Stanmer, and re-elected in May 2019. In early 2021 I moved away for family reasons and stepped down, having served for almost six years. I spent quite a lot of those six years wondering why so many people who didn't know me seemed to hate me so much. Compared to some of my colleagues, I got away lightly: I wasn't trolled on social media, I wasn't stalked and I didn't get death threats. But it was always there, that hesitation you can feel when you explain who you are, the avoidance tactics, the habit of always assuming the worst.

Like many politicians, I knocked on a lot of doors, and I have also done so to support other campaigns. While most people on the doorstep are polite, I often feel it's because they're holding back. Then there are those who make it clear they don't want to know, like a gentleman last December who slammed the door once I'd introduced myself, and went back to putting up Christmas decorations in his front window. Or the woman who went to take the dog inside when I showed up at the gate, and then stayed inside herself until I went away. Then there was the person (I never actually saw them) who was hoovering when I put a councillor's newsletter through the door. The hoover stopped and, seconds later as I walked away, the door opened and the scrunched-up leaflet rolled past me down the garden path. As well as this canvassing equivalent of the silent treatment, pretty much every door-knocking session features someone who says, with emotions ranging from boredom to sheer incandescent rage, that they aren't interested in politics, that they don't bother with it, that there's no point, because "you're all the same!".

It's no surprise why so many think this. An alien from another galaxy, conducting research on Earth's system of government through examining our public discourse, could only conclude that politicians are a bunch of contemptible incompetents who invariably screw things up and have little in the way of moral fibre. The alien might also be curious as to why we choose such terrible people for the job. Why don't we just choose different people? Well, we quite often do – and end up hating them just as much. This book is my view on why this is, and why it's so damaging.

Here's an example of how entrenched this is. A few years ago I saw a post on Facebook which listed an alarming number of offences apparently committed by MPs. Here is a more recent version from fullfact.org[ii], exactly as it appears there:

"Can you imagine working for a company that only has a little more than 635 employees, but has the following employee statistics.. 29 have been accused of spouse abuse 7 have been arrested for fraud… 9 have been accused of writing bad cheques … 17 have directly or indirectly bankrupted at least 2 businesses 3 have done time for assault 71 cannot get a credit card due to bad credit 14 have been arrested on drug-related charges 8 have been arrested for shoplifting 21 are currently defendants in lawsuits 84 have been arrested for drink driving in the last year AND Collectively, this year alone, have cost the British tax payer £92,993,748 in expenses! Which organisation is this? You guessed it, it's the HOUSE OF COMMONS"

As fullfact makes clear, this post is false. It's been around for twenty years, surfacing in different parts of the world with slightly altered figures. In its original form it claimed to be describing the US House of Representatives, but none of the figures in it could be substantiated and the same numbers have simply been used globally over and over again.

Now when I first saw this post, it was the alarmingly large number of MPs arrested for drink driving that got me suspicious: in the version above, 84 in a single year. That's more than one arrest per week, all year long. It's more than the total number of Lib Dem, SNP, DUP and Sinn Fein members in the current parliament put together. In fact it's more than all the opposition MPs put together except Labour. It's absurd. And yet a number of my friends and contacts shared this post and commented along the lines that they weren't surprised at all.

Have any MPs been done for drink driving? One or two over the years, judging from a rudimentary Google search. Chris Huhne was caught out trying to dodge a speeding charge in 2003. That was serious enough to lead to his resignation and a by-election. MPs, and politicians everywhere, are certainly not perfect. But we have a problem if large numbers of citizens think that all politicians are venal, vain, incompetent, arrogant and dishonest, as opposed to just some of them.

Here's Ricky Gervais on YouTube in December 2021[iii], colourfully addressing the topic of Partygate:

"The fucking people in charge do what they want…I see all these people saying…all the parties they were having, all the stuff they were doing…the people in charge, the posh, privileged people in charge were acting like fucking Charlie Sheen. I mean, really fucking rubbing salt into the wound…I don't get political, but they're all wankers. When are we going to stop taking 'went to Eton' as a qualification to run the country?"

The anger is understandable, and the language might be forgivable – but the generalisation? All of them? Really?

This isn't a rhetorical one-off. Focus group research conducted across England in 2021 by Renaissance Labour[iv] reveals that "trust in political parties is virtually non-existent", and "confidence is undermined by two core beliefs…politicians are self-interested [and] full of empty promises". This is what people actually said:

- "Labour and the Conservatives are the same. They're in it to line their own pockets and their friends."
- "All parties are in it for themselves – they just want your vote."
- "They are full of promises to try to keep everyone happy but they just tell lies."
- "They all promise you everything, then turn up with a barrel full of mud."

I think it would be fair to describe these sentiments as somewhat sweeping. Explicitly so: these people mean everybody, and say so. We see the same view reflected in the world of fiction. Whenever a TV show or a novel features an elected politician of any status, they're bound to be up to something, whether they're in bed with big business, in bed with their secretary, or involved in a clandestine society that goes about anything from child abuse to the clubbing of small furry animals. If it's a murder mystery, there isn't much mystery: head straight to the politician to find the buried corpse. For variation, sometimes it's the aide, adviser or partner who does the deed, but however it plays out the representative in question never comes across well.

Who remembers *The West Wing*, the fabulous Aaron Sorkin saga featuring Martin Sheen as the best president the USA never had? This show is, apparently, naïve and unrealistic. TV critic Heather Havrilesky is quoted on

Wikipedia[v] as saying "What rock did these morally pure creatures crawl out from under and, more important, how do you go from innocent millipede to White House staffer without becoming soiled or disillusioned by the dirty realities of politics along the way?" But I don't think this is the case. The characters are not paragons of virtue, and the storylines feature plenty of dirty realities. All kinds of shenanigans play out around political alliances and there's a good deal of campaigning pragmatism. The President hides the fact that he has a chronic illness in order to get elected. At one point he authorises the summary assassination of a terror suspect on foreign soil. This is hardly "morally pure". So why are they described as such? It's because the characters (aside from being unfeasibly attractive, I'll concede that) are well-intentioned, essentially good people trying to do the right thing. They are not bad people, although they sometimes do bad, or at least questionable, things. To me this seems utterly realistic. But by today's standards it's too saccharine to be believed. Because politicians aren't like that, are they?

Let's take a step back and consider who we're talking about. The House of Commons consists of 650 MPs, but we have more politicians than that. According to the Local Government Information Unit[vi] there are 398 principal councils across the UK, and on top of that around 11,300 parish or town councils. If we assume that there are, let's say, 50 councillors on each local authority and 11 on each parish council, that would give us 144,200 local councillors. Allowing for vacancies and seats at different levels to be held by the same person, this would reduce it down a little, but we're still talking about well over a hundred thousand. That's an awful lot of "wankers", as Gervais put it. Can it ever be justifiable to generalise in such negative terms – or indeed in any terms – about such large numbers of people?

I don't mean you, I've heard people say. I mean the people at the top, those at Number Ten and so on. The people in charge, as Gervais said. The political coverage most people hear about most of the time is focused on a very small number of people at Westminster. While opinions improve closer to home, they're still not especially favourable: a 2021 YouGov survey for Carnegie UK[vii] found that only 17% trusted MPs, 20% trusted the UK government and 32% trusted local government "to make decisions that will improve your life and the lives of people like you". Research by Ipsos-MORI for the Local Government Association[viii] shows that local councillors and local government are more trusted than national politicians, but overall levels are still low across the board. This pervades everything, local and national, and is a massive hurdle when trying to communicate with the electorate. The hooverer-bowler who tossed my newsletter after me didn't stop to consider whether anyone featured in the leaflet was local or national. Local politicians are still politicians after all, most of us aligned to one party or another, standing on the values and reputation of that party as much as, if not more than, our own.

I challenge people, naturally. We're really not all the same, I point out. We have different policies. Different values. Different records in power. Quite often people concede this. But it doesn't matter, they counter, because you don't deliver anything anyway. What's the point in having values and policies when nothing ever changes? So really, they don't mean that we're all the same. What they mean is, we're all equally crap.

Not much of a comfort, I know. Maybe it just comes with the job, some have argued. Politicians have power. That's bound to make them unpopular some of the time: inevitably they will make unpopular decisions. I've had jovial conversations with people who are perfectly fine with me while at the same time laughingly dismissing our entire political establishment: "Johnson? He's an idiot! But then so's Starmer! And the rest of 'em!" Agreeing with one or more of the above is understandable, if a little strong, but agreeing with all three is problematic, if it's widespread (and I think it is): it suggests that the problem isn't some underperformance within the democratic structure, but the structure itself.

Maybe they're just letting off steam. Sometimes these sentiments express a general frustration and hyperbole that dissipates if there's an opportunity for meaningful conversation. It's also "socially safe" to slag off politicians: others will generally agree with you and you won't end up in the middle of a slanging match about Brexit, or having to defend things you don't want to defend. But there are plenty – like those in the focus groups – who are adamant that the entire political class is good for nothing. This is a problem because they're not discriminating between good politicians and bad ones, which is the key role of the citizen in a democracy. Many don't even vote. And then we're in a downward spiral: the fewer there are who take part, the fewer feel ownership of the decisions being made on their behalf, and this is the whole point of democracy.

The danger is that politicians end up being resented by their electorate not because of anything about themselves or anything they've done, but simply because they're politicians. We can't have a democracy without elected representatives. Yet a sizeable proportion of citizens don't feel that the electoral method of choosing representatives assures their trust. Quite the opposite, in fact. As a result, decisions are made without the participation of large sections of society. Eventually, these sentiments could lead to a rejection of democracy entirely in favour of something that just feels a lot easier. It's happened before: it could happen again.

Can we change this? Can we get to a better place, where politicians can be identified as good or bad (or at least better or worse), as opposed to universally bad? My view is that the negativity with which politicians are viewed is partly – but only partly – their own fault, and it isn't entirely within the gift of politicians to fix it. This may be controversial, but democracy isn't simply something that's dispensed from above. It's a machine consisting of moving parts, and requires participation from multiple stakeholders – commentators and opinion-formers, news reporters and editors, anyone with a role in civic society and the community, and voters themselves – in order to work properly.

I can't offer some masterplan. What I can do is give a flavour of what it's like to be a politician, making decisions in the face of competing voices, limited options, shrinking budgets and multiple demands on one's time. I can share a personal perspective on where this negativity springs from, and I can provide examples of the positive achievements of politicians in order to make some small attempt to right the balance. I'm not trying to stifle criticism, debate or accountability. I'd be happy enough if the "all" heard everywhere, either implied or stated, were replaced at times with "some". Because whatever else politicians are, we're definitely not all the same.

We're Not All the Same

2. They're Out of Touch

"Hi! I'm your local councillor. Any issues?"

"My local councillor, eh? Well, *I've* never seen you before."

"Well, I live in the ward. Just a few minutes away."

"Never seen you up here."

"We knocked in this street a few months ago."

"Well, you didn't come here."

"Maybe you were out."

"I don't go out."

"Didn't hear the bell?"

"I always hear the bell."

"We'd have left a calling card."

Blank look. "Nope."

I could have added that we leafleted every home multiple times during the recent election, that we have a column in the local community newsletter and do drop-in surgeries, that we're on Facebook and Twitter, that our contact details are on the council's website and elsewhere online, and that we attend numerous local events and community meetings. In short, we did everything we could think of to inform our residents that we were there and wanted to hear from them. As a consequence, a lot of people got in touch and we tried to help them with a huge variety of different matters. But among the many more that we didn't reach, when we managed to make contact, some were minded to be hostile right from the get-go.

I don't expect everyone in the country to know who their local councillors are. Until I became actively involved in politics, I certainly didn't. I didn't know which party ran the local council, and I wouldn't always have been able to name my MP, either. It was my choice not to take more of an interest.

Local politics doesn't float everyone's boat, and if most people most of the time don't have any burning issues, that's no bad thing. In fact, not knowing who your local councillor is might be considered a good thing. It probably means that there hasn't been a planning application you haven't liked, cars aren't parked all over the pavement, no one has left a fridge on the grass verge and the bins have been emptied. All is well! That's the most common response I get on the doorstep when asking for issues. But what strikes me about conversations like that above, along with similar comments on social media, is a tendency for residents to assume that if they have heard nothing about their elected representatives, then those representatives aren't doing anything. From my side, it felt like we were going out of our way to get our names out, providing multiple means of getting in touch. If people didn't, I wouldn't have had a problem with it. Nevertheless, those who weren't aware of us often seemed to default to a negative opinion about who we were and what we were doing for them. Given the nature of political commentary generally, this is hardly surprising.

Politicians are out of touch, it's often said. They don't live in the real world. They have no idea what ordinary folk are going through. They're elsewhere, distant, off living some privileged life somewhere. That is undoubtedly true of some: at times a politician will say or do something that suggests they live in a totally different world from that of their constituents. However, of all the politicians that I've known – across all parties – most generally go to great lengths to try and stay in touch with their constituents.

In our case, in a marginal ward, we got to know our residents through the election campaigns themselves. This involved systematically working round every street to speak to as many as possible, plus leaflets, social media posts and so on. Once elected, it's a matter of trying to find the time to do all the work you've been elected to do plus retain a reasonable level of contact. This is true at all levels. Local councillors have to balance the time they spend in their wards with other commitments, often work. MPs have to be in London a certain amount of the time. It requires dedication and effort to door-knock regularly, regardless of what else is going on. Even for those who succeed, it's quite a job to get round everybody.

My ward, represented by three councillors, had roughly 12,000 residents living in around 8,000 households. Within a weekly door-knocking session of 1.5 to two hours, given the number of people who are out at any time, one person might speak to around fifteen residents. In a good session this might go up to twenty. Let's take the highest number: twenty contacts in two hours gives us ten per hour. So the total amount of door-knocking we'd need to speak to someone in every household would be 800 hours. A team of three would need 133 sessions. That's once a week for just over two years.

This isn't how it works, because so many people are out so much of the time. To speak to the people who are often out involves going back repeatedly at different times of the day and week, an effort only possible during by-elections and in very marginal seats when volunteers can be pulled in from elsewhere. Added to this, my working theory is that only about fifty percent of the nation's doorbells work. With buzzers, it's surely less (how do these people get parcels?). In one part of the ward I became convinced that the perennially low contact rates were due to the fact that most flats had an outer door and an inner door (and no buzzers), and people simply couldn't hear us knocking.

In normal times, getting round the entire ward with a handful of helpers doing a regular session would take at the very least a few months. It all speeds up at election time of course. But that's just one ward. My parliamentary constituency consisted of seven wards. If the MP doorknocked single-handedly, it would, theoretically, take them over forty years to speak to everyone. No one does that, of course. MPs will aim to recruit teams of volunteers to come out and help them. Even so, getting round everyone is a big undertaking.

While some residents are never in, with other households you tend to speak to the same people each time. In multi-generational households it's often the older generation, with sons and daughters at work, out, away, or just in the middle of something. Other homes have new residents in them every time. In my patch a sizeable student population added to the churn: almost as soon as they appear on the register they're looking to move again. And a long and involved conversation with an individual, while usually very worthwhile, will result in a dramatic reduction in number of contacts that week.

"You only come round at election time" is a frequent observation of world-weary electors. But this is why it might seem that way. Constituencies are big, and people are out. Even with the best will in the world, many people aren't going to see their MP standing at the front door that often. Councillors slightly more so, but to get any traction requires volunteers ready to give up their time. Like many others, I've done this very thing in numerous elections, by-elections and campaigns over the years. There's nothing like speaking to people directly to hear what folk are really thinking. But our numbers are limited, which is why parties focus so strenuously on marginal seats, and multiply the effort so significantly in the run-up to an election. Next time someone says we need fewer MPs – following the general sentiment of the fewer the better – bear in mind that fewer MPs will inevitably mean larger constituencies (and the same for local councillors and their wards), and elected representatives spread more thinly across a greater number of residents. It may save money (though it won't necessarily result in less casework), but at a price.

Many residents contact their local councillors or MP directly to raise a specific issue. There are many more who don't. When constituents air the commonly-held view that all politicians are out of touch, I sometimes try and ask if they've had any direct dealings with their local representatives. If they have, and got no response or one that they didn't like, they have cause for complaint. But some of the most incensed haven't actually tried, often out of a preconception that there'll be "no point". Well, I'm here now, I sometimes say. An entire door-knocking session is justified whenever this persuades a disaffected constituent to rethink.

Those who have had some dealings with politicians will have more time for them, it seems to me. They may well have a better experience of some than others, but that's natural and normal. What isn't natural or normal – or shouldn't be – is when all politicians are equally and emphatically dismissed, primarily by those who are not particularly engaged, who are responding to the dominant tone with which politics is discussed rather than from any direct experience.

Another aspect of "They're out of touch" is the idea that politicians are part of a well-heeled elite, a political aristocracy. Ricky Gervais pointed the finger at "the posh, privileged people in charge". He was probably mainly talking about the Cabinet or the PM's office, but his words threw the net a lot wider, as they often do. These days, it's said, they're all university-educated and middle-class: career politicians fresh out of Oxbridge via Eton, former special advisers, cocooned in their ivory tower with their posh cars and their second homes. They just don't experience the hard knocks of life.

Again, this may well be true of some MPs, but it certainly isn't true of all of them. Plenty have gone on record talking about difficult childhoods and lives that have seen more than a fair share of tragedy and adversity. From the Labour benches, John Prescott, Alan Johnson and Jess Phillips spring to mind. There's also the famous pair of bus drivers' sons, Sadiq Khan and Sajid Javid. That said, taken as a whole, the demographic background of MPs is more skewed towards graduates and those with professional careers behind them. If this is a problem it needs to be addressed by looking at why it's happening. In the meantime I don't myself go along with the idea that someone who has that background can't prove to be a good politician. As a graduate with a professional background myself, I would defend my involvement in politics. I know I've only walked one path in life, and to understand the experiences of others I need to reach out and be prepared to listen. Empathy is key. It's also important to be part of an inclusive team and work successfully together. But that's true for all politicians, regardless of background.

Is this perception only for parliamentary MPs? I don't think so. It's all right for *you*, someone might say to one of us, opposing a local planning application. How would *you* like it if your garden were overlooked, or a ton of new people came to live in your area, or you couldn't park anywhere any more? The implication was that we councillors were unaffected by such things, making it all the more frustrating when we made decisions that affected others. For reference, my garden was already overlooked, the population density in my area was pretty high already, numerous planning applications were passed during the time I lived there, and as for the parking – more on that later. Councillors were just as likely to be impacted by planning decisions as anybody else, but this didn't fit with the idea of politicians as an uncaring elite.

A volunteer at a local church contacted me to complain that he was no longer able to use the recycling bins outside the church, as they were intended only for residents. What were we supposed to do? he asked. I told him about a general recycling point nearby, at the far end of a car park that was right opposite the church. It would use too much petrol, he said, to drive there. I gave my opinion that since he drove to the church anyway, an additional fifty yards would make little difference to his motoring costs. His response: "I'd like to have *your* salary." But what did he know about my salary? Faced with hearing something he didn't much like, he objected to it by making assumptions about my income, based on the widely-perpetuated belief that all politicians are wealthy.

Amongst the local politicians and candidates I've known personally, I can think of more than one call centre worker, a salesman, at least one single mum, airline cabin crew, a teacher, a nurse, a shop owner, and plenty doing ungenerously-paid jobs in the voluntary or public sector. Some had first-hand experience of poverty, homelessness and social exclusion, mental health issues, tragic bereavement, ill-health and financial insecurity. In fact it was often these experiences which prompted them to go into politics in the first place. There were also those, including me, with professional or managerial backgrounds; such a mix of experiences seemed healthy to me.

None of this was a secret: councillors had to declare their occupation. If residents wanted some idea of what kind of background their representatives had, they could always ask, but I don't recall this happening very much. Instead, the general perception of politicians tended to prevail, particularly when difficult decisions were being made, or when we needed to say things folk didn't want to hear.

Democracy isn't just for election time. During a politician's whole term of office, constituents can make their views known, ask them for help, see what they're doing, look up how they're voting, hold them to account for all they do. Many constituents do just that. But many more do not, thus narrowing active participation in a system specifically there to enable ordinary people to have some say in how things are done. This is at least in part due to the image of the elite, distanced politician who isn't going to be interested in ordinary lives, and prevents many from taking steps to find out whether their representatives really do care or not.

Could politicians be more in touch, and better represent their constituents in terms of their background and experiences? Yes, for sure. As we'll see in the next chapter, it isn't that easy to persuade people to go into politics, and our democracy misses out as a result. But making generalisations or assumptions – which some politicians do themselves at times to score an easy point over an opponent – is not in the interests of anyone in the longer term. The links between the elected and those they work for are weakened, and the benefits of our democratic system are not realised as they should be. In the resultant disconnect, someone coming along claiming to be able to do better for people than all this elections and voting nonsense may end up being listened to far more than they deserve.

We're Not All the Same

3. They Don't Keep their Promises

In our 2015 manifesto for Brighton and Hove, Labour promised to build 500 new council homes. At the end of four years, we'd just about got up to 200. We tried for the full 500, but it was more difficult than we thought it would be for a variety of reasons: companies going bust, delays with planning permission and other internal decisions, opposition from local residents, staff shortage and absence, ever-increasing costs.

Could we have done better? Probably, though I wasn't close enough to the nuts and bolts to say exactly how. It could also have been worse. Could we have managed the entire 500? I don't think so, and I don't think another party could have done, either.

Was it an empty promise to start with? It certainly wasn't. It was largely based on a pipeline that was already there. In theory we just needed to carry it out as planned. In practice, there's a big difference between a list in a spreadsheet and a series of complex projects that only ever diminished in size and grew in difficulty. But we certainly intended to do it and put some considerable effort into trying.

So we didn't keep our promise. Having said all that, 200 isn't bad. It compared pretty well to direct delivery by councils elsewhere in the country. It meant good quality homes for residents on our waiting lists at affordable council rents and pretty secure tenancies. That 200 made a difference to many more hundreds of people locally. It wasn't nothing, by any means.

Should politicians be credited for getting halfway there, or in our case 40%? I think so. No one should be promising something they know can't be achieved. But setting a stretch target that's doable and managing to get part way there ought to be recognised for what it is. Many of us in our lives have wonderful intentions that never actually come off: look at gym membership every January. Our expectations of politicians are higher than that, and rightly so. But can they sometimes be too high?

I was only out leafletting when I met my top contender for Mr Angry. He really was the angriest man I've ever spoken to, furious that I'd had the temerity to post something through his letterbox, and he came out to thrust it back into my hand.

"You're a worthless bunch of scoundrels!" he said (I'm paraphrasing). "NONE of you have EVER done ANYTHING! It's ALL LIES!"

"What, never?" I ventured.

"NEVER!"

"None of us?"

"NONE of you!"

I should have just walked away, but that's difficult sometimes. Maybe there was some specific reason for his ire. Maybe he could be persuaded to concede something. Eventually I asked him if he'd personally ever set out to do something but not achieved it. His answer was a categorical no.

"What, never?" I ventured again.

"NEVER!"

It would be nice to be that sure of anything in life. My answer would certainly have been yes. But I'm confident I'm not the only one, and I don't regret having tried in the first place. A consequence of only awarding points to politicians if they achieve 100% of their targets is that it's quite a strong incentive to avoid ambitious targets. But as long as they are still achievable, ambitious targets can really help to mobilise and make things happen. Even if the target eventually isn't met, the result can be positive. However, a positive result often seems to get lost in the narrative of a broken promise.

If anything less than 100% success is failure, this blunts the ability to distinguish between political parties, individuals and approaches that deliver and those that don't. By this standard, if we'd only managed a hundred council homes, or got up to 400, it's all the same: we still didn't meet our target. But the difference between 100 and 400 new homes within a four-year period is huge. Turning politics into a game of absolutes might seem to simplify, but in fact makes it difficult to tell the good from the bad, or, more accurately, the better from the worse.

It would be easy for our political opponents to claim that they would have delivered more housing than us. One of the difficulties with evaluating political performance is that there is no way of knowing that for sure. Unless we divided the city into two and conducted some kind of enormous split test, the situation in which one party is operating is never going to be exactly the same as that during which the other side gets a go. Circumstances constantly change, but taking this into account is difficult, as a party defending its record by explaining the limitations can sound like it's making excuses, and the opposition will surely accuse them of that. Perhaps it's understandable that some voters trying to prise all this messaging apart conclude that they're all as bad as each other. But ultimately, the voter's role is to listen to the arguments and exercise an element of judgement: that's the very purpose of democracy.

Sometimes a promise wasn't even a promise in the first place. Between 2011 and 2015 when the Greens were in control for the first time, Labour secured a budget amendment to release a small amount of money to investigate the possibility of doorstep food waste collection. An investigation was duly done – but Labour then voted against the pilot scheme that was proposed. Labour was accused of backtracking – presenting itself as "pro caddy" but then blocking it.

Why the change of mind? Because the investigation gave some indication of the costs involved in rolling out doorstep collection across the city, and no means of funding had been identified (by the administration) to cover this. Other recycling-related initiatives were considered higher priority for what funding there was. What's the point in a pilot when the money isn't there to roll it out? A pilot's meant to be a precursor, a testbed for something bigger that's launching afterwards. A one-off with no follow-up wouldn't have been worth paying for. To put the money into context, the cost of the investigation was tens of thousands. A pilot would be hundreds of thousands. Rolling out an actual food waste scheme would have come to millions. Labour did not "promise" food waste collection. It promised (in this case by securing the funding for) an investigation, and if, as a result of the investigation the whole idea seemed unviable, we had promised nothing further. But that didn't stop it being presented by our opponents as a rollback on a promise.

Weasel words? Designed to sound bigger and better than anything that could be delivered? Or is there an important distinction between undertaking to investigate a new service and promising to actually deliver it? Most manifestos I've seen have been carefully worded in this way, and quite often don't make that many out-and-out promises. We say that we will "work hard towards" something, to "prioritise" it, to "support" it. For a party in opposition looking to come in and take power (particularly after a long gap), it's difficult to be that certain about what you can deliver. This probably sounds terribly weak, but it's true nevertheless. Those promises that weren't kept, much of the time they were never made in the first place.

Ever read your travel insurance policy? They're a masterclass in weasel words, if you want to look at it like that. To take just one example, how does my policy define "close relative"? This is in the context of paying out if you have to return because something bad happens to one. Turns out that aunts and uncles aren't considered close relatives. Up and down the generational ladder is okay – grandparents and grandchildren – and in-laws count (some of them), as do step relatives and foster carers and children, but not nephews and nieces. One could make a fuss, but the truth is, these companies fall over themselves to tell you to read the small print, and their product and its pricing is based on what they cover and what they don't. We know they don't cover everything. So what about politics? Do we accept that politicians can deliver some things but not others? I wonder about this. We might sweat over the wording of a manifesto commitment in order to avoid over-promising, but often this doesn't seem to count for much in the general reckoning.

There are some who think it's inevitable in a modern democracy that expectations are high and opinions low. These are two sides of the same coin: if expectations could somehow be reined in, it might become a little more feasible for politicians to meet them more often, and therefore be judged a little less harshly. This can sometimes be discussed effectively on the doorstep, by explaining the limitations. However, expectations seem to develop a consciousness of their own, growing over time, evolving from when they were first conceived.

This is particularly the case when a party is in opposition. The more time the expectations have to grow, the bigger they get, expanding to fill the vacuum of powerlessness. In the wilderness years prior to 1997, expectations of what a Labour government would do once in power had a very long time to mature. For many, once Blair's government was in, the disappointment was fast and acute. "It wasn't socialism," a woman in Brighton told me on the doorstep, in the run-up to the 2010 general election. She'd formed this view within a year or two of Labour's landslide victory. While we could write an entire book about what she might have meant by socialism, I bet most of what she envisaged wasn't in the manifesto. Those who have analysed the performance of Labour in government – including, for example, Polly Toynbee and David Walker in *Did Things Get Better?* (2001) – thought that they actually delivered quite a lot of what was promised. But for some, it came nowhere near the heights that their expectations had reached.

Other types of profession don't seem to get this. If a doctor treated someone for cancer, but the worst happened and the cancer came back, would there be anger directed at the doctor and their team? I think most would accept that those involved in the treatment did the best they could. What's critical is that the doctor and others managed expectations well. The patient needs an accurate idea of how likely it is that the treatment will work. The doctor is only expected to deliver what the medical profession is able to – and when they explain what that is, and what can and can't be done, they're believed.

Politicians have a more difficult job here. For one thing, they have to be elected. This requires them to present themselves positively across a wide range of policy areas to thousands, or indeed millions, of people, many of whom don't have much time or inclination to absorb the detail. Politicians have to stand for something. What would *you* do, the electorate wants to know. So politicians make promises and pledges that demonstrate their values. It sometimes feels like a trap: electors are agog for politicians to tell them what they want to hear – but one of the key criticisms of politicians is that they're too eager to do just that.

Remember Clegg and his 2012 tuition fee pledge apology? Actually he didn't apologise for breaking the Liberal Democrats' 2010 pledge to scrap university tuition fees: he apologised for having made the pledge in the first place. As a smaller party and only able to govern as part of a coalition, he said, the Lib Dems should have been more honest with the electorate about what they could achieve in power, because everything would be the result of a negotiation with their coalition partners. He's right, but what politicians are also expected to do is present a vision of the future which is inspirational, or at least noticeable, in order to win an election. This is a difficult path to tread. While staying within the realms of the possible, we need to put our values on display and show voters how we're different. We have to generate excitement and enthusiasm while also remaining relevant and credible. If we don't do this, we won't win. If we're not trying to win, then we're not really serious about being politicians.

One of the problems with expectations of politics is that very little is out of scope. A doctor is only expected to treat things medical, according to their specialism. But politics can include pretty much anything. MPs can legislate: this gives them a lot of power, at least in theory. Local councillors have a specific role in the decisions and operations of their council, but there's more to it than that. Councils and councillors also engage in "civic leadership" and play an influencing role that goes way beyond their constitutional remit.

Contact us if you have any problems, councillors sometimes say, admittedly throwing the net very wide. A former colleague claims that someone showed up at her surgery once with a broken carpet sweeper and asked her to fix it. She obligingly did. The same resident came back later with a surgical corset. Luckily, he wasn't wearing it at the time. When asking people if they have any local issues, they really could come up with anything. They might, for example, ask about some piece of land that's been sitting derelict for ages. The simplest reply, if the land is privately owned, is that it's ultimately down to the landowner to maintain it, bring forward some plans to develop it, or sell it on. However, in all these cases there may be something I could do as a councillor. The council may have some powers to encourage the owners to act. We might need to start talking about compulsory purchase orders. We could have meetings. We could lobby. We could propose some kind of partnership and see about applying for funding. I could think of some other way to put pressure on the relevant people on behalf of my constituents. So the lines aren't drawn as clearly as they might be in other areas. But this is all about trying to influence something over which I have no direct control. While I can promise to act, I can be less certain of the results.

Another example would be something like health inequality. One of the annual public health reports produced while I was in post made some startling comparisons between the life expectancy of residents at one end of the Number One bus route compared with those at the other. Public health is very much on the agenda for local councils, but within it falls a huge raft of behaviour and decisions over which the council has no direct control. Brighton and Hove's Health and Wellbeing Strategy[ix] talks about the importance of partnership working, which is just as well, as many of its aims simply can't be delivered by the council acting alone. The strategy's objectives span all ages and include immunisation rates for babies, eating, drinking and smoking habits for adults, falls prevention amongst the elderly and ensuring people have more choice about where they die. It's a good strategy and its success will do much to improve lives across the city, but much of it is about communications and influencing behaviour. When people say that politicians promise the world and only deliver a barrel of mud, are they expecting social problems like health inequality to be solved by politicians alone? If so, no wonder they're disappointed.

Sometimes promises aren't kept purely because in time things change. While there's a public appetite to see things happen quickly, the work of politicians is often slow and long term. Goalposts move in the meantime. Another commitment Labour made to Brighton and Hove in 2015 was to build a new secondary school. When we came into power in that year, the numbers were up and it was difficult to see how all pupils were going to be accommodated. We got to work but problems cropped up. One was that a local authority no longer has the power to open a new school, thanks to government legislation. Our only option was to find someone who would sponsor an academy or set up a free school. This made the whole idea unpopular with many within the education community who were not keen on the non-local-authority models. We pressed on, as these models were all that was available, but finding a site was also problematic. In the meantime a growing number of pupils were not offered a place at their schools of choice, and this kicked off some noisy campaigns.

Then two things happened. Firstly, two of the most popular schools in the city did a sudden about-face and, after years of saying they had no more space to take on more pupils, announced that they could, given the right funding and so on. Secondly, the birth rate dropped. After a few years of high numbers, the pattern looked set to reverse and the need would fall off. Given all of this, it seemed foolish to continue, so we abandoned the idea. A promise not met, but for good reasons.

Another situation in which politicians don't keep their promises is when they change their minds. When Labour was in opposition to the Green council of 2011-2015, there was a plan to reduce the subsidy to some of the city's bus services. This was, to be fair, in the context of local government funding cuts – but these particular proposals would have left some parts of the city without a viable comprehensive bus service, with plenty in peak hours but none at all on a Sunday evening, for example (I know that's normal in much of the country, but Brighton and Hove is blessed with good buses). There was a vigorous campaign, in which I played a role. The Greens caved in. They did a U-turn. They rowed back. They made an embarrassing climb-down. And all the other words that are used when politicians change their minds.

It's a time for great hand-rubbing amongst political commentators when this happens nationally. Only last week, someone will point out, the minister was saying this! Now they're saying that! Well, that's kind of how it works. Is it a weakness to change your mind? Inadequacy? Incompetence? It certainly sounds like it sometimes. But do we really want to be governed by people who never, ever change their minds about anything? Politicians are meant to listen, aren't they (see "They Don't Listen")? What if people are telling them their idea sucks? Wouldn't it then be a good thing for them to act on it?

No politician, or political party, can guarantee that every plan they make will be problem-free. One of the reasons why government has to go through a process of consultation before making changes is to give people an opportunity to point out what the consequences might be. Shouldn't politicians be ready to hear this and take it on board if their proposals aren't going down as well as they'd assumed? They should have anticipated, you might say; they should have known it was a bad idea. It's certainly true that some ideas have been proposed that should never have seen the light of day. But equally, expecting politicians to get it right all the time doesn't sound realistic.

Changing one's mind in response to campaigning, lobbying or simply the strength of public opinion is often the right thing to do. This may not apply when addressing some age-old problem that gets kicked back into the long grass year after year: in my time, supported accommodation for rough sleepers, inequitable school catchment areas and controversial development sites were a few. But at other times politicians should be thanked for changing their minds.

To return to the bigger point: is the general cynicism about politicians and their promises really about only delivering 200 homes when we said 500? I sometimes think there's a general promise out there that's never articulated but which all politicians in a democracy have been signed up to by default. It's the idea that things are always going to keep getting better, that we'll each of us always have more, that we'll never lose anything we've already got, that the problems of the world can be fixed without any tangible price being paid. It may not be a promise that's ever crossed the lips of a politician, but it's what's being heard by electors. Opposition messaging and journalistic commentary adds to this over time by highlighting the shortcomings and downsides of whatever is on the table, as if politicians should somehow always find a positive way forward that never brings with it a negative. But that's a promise none of us can keep.

4. They're Always Bickering

We're Not All the Same

"Why can't you all just get together to sort things out?" This was a common sentiment door-knocking in the May 2021 local elections as the world battled the pandemic. Like you did during World War Two, more than one person said, referring to the coalition government of that time. Instead, they complained, you're busy arguing with each other.

Given the way politics is reported and discussed, I get why people think this. But to a large extent, I tried to say, that's exactly what we are doing. And not just during a pandemic, but all the time.

Brighton and Hove City Council is a three-way marginal – Conservative, Labour and Green – with a committee system. No party has had overall control since before 2003. This means that whichever party leads, every decision the council makes has to be backed by one or other of the opposition parties. Every decision is a cross-party decision: if the opposition parties wanted to stop something happening, they could vote together against it (they could do this for very different reasons, of course). While this is hard work and involves a large amount of officer time, decisions do get made and business gets done. It didn't always feel particularly constructive, but if the parties didn't "work together" at all, decision-making would effectively stop.

There was more common ground than you might think. Take the annual budget, for example, the most important vote of the year. Once the leading party proposes the budget, a set process is followed by which opposition parties can propose amendments – which then have to be costed – and are voted on during the course of what's normally a very long meeting and which in itself is the culmination of at least four months of discussion and negotiation. But these amendments rarely affect more than 5% of the total budget being proposed. Often they are for very small amounts indeed. A hundred thousand pounds here, fifty thousand there, and yes, in the context of a budget of eight hundred million, that is a small amount. The rest of it is simply agreed, after a great deal of scrutiny and analysis. But that's not the impression you'd get from reading the press coverage which, understandably enough, focuses on the areas of contention.

Submerged beneath the public debate lies an iceberg of hidden agreement: while each party has its own priorities and values, they all have a huge amount in common when it comes to what they want for the city. Pleasant, prosperous, affordable, safe, sustainable, fair – these were all desirable aims that we held in common. When opposition parties took issue with our proposals, often it was not about what we wanted to do, but how we were going to do it.

Here's how an Iceberg of Agreement in Brighton and Hove in around 2020-2021 might look:

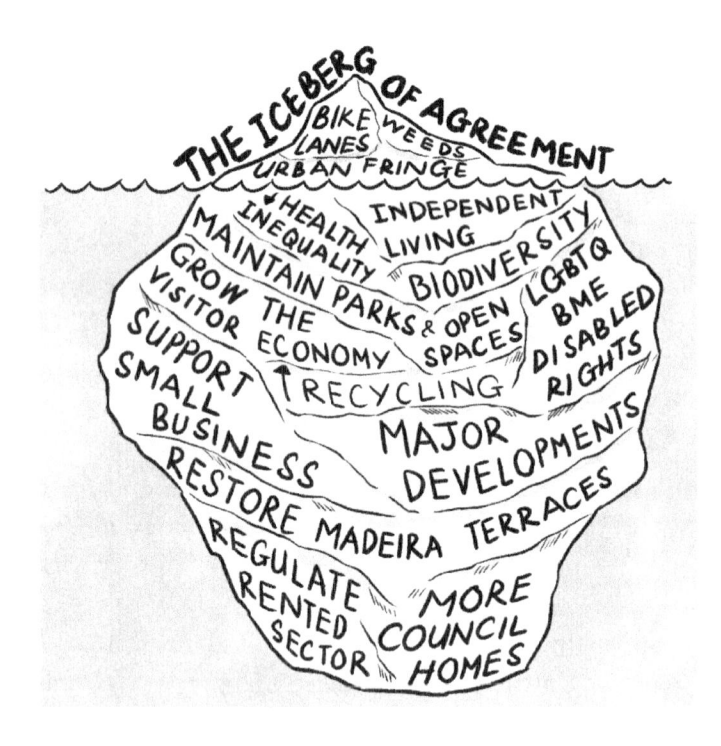

THE ICEBERG OF AGREEMENT
BIKE LANES
WEEDS
URBAN FRINGE

HEALTH INEQUALITY
INDEPENDENT LIVING
MAINTAIN PARKS & OPEN SPACES
BIODIVERSITY
LGBTQ
BME
GROW THE VISITOR ECONOMY
DISABLED RIGHTS
SUPPORT SMALL BUSINESS
RECYCLING
MAJOR DEVELOPMENTS
RESTORE MADEIRA TERRACES
REGULATE RENTED SECTOR
MORE COUNCIL HOMES

Take council housing, for example. Generally, everyone wanted to see new council housing built on council land: it was a cost-effective way of delivering high quality and genuinely affordable homes. Our proposals often stalled in committee, though. To massively simplify, this was because the Tories thought we were building too expensive and the Greens thought we were charging too much rent. I have distilled many, many hours of discussion into that one sentence. It's all on the council's website if you want chapter and verse[x].

Negotiating all these objections to move forward cost a lot in terms of officer time and resources, as plans were revised and follow-up meetings rescheduled. Opposition leads were often proud that they influenced a proposal and managed to shave significant amounts off the proposed costs, or the proposed rents. With their contribution, arguably, what went forward was stronger because they, having been democratically elected to do so, influenced things in line with their values.

It could have been easier, though. Instead of raising these objections at the earliest possible opportunity during a scheduled confidential briefing, in time for their ideas to be incorporated into the committee proposal, they waited until everything was in the public domain before they started to criticise it. Why? For the headlines. Without those, people wouldn't have known what they stood for. The parties "bickered", if you like, in public, quite unnecessarily, because had they not done so, they would have struggled to get the kind of media exposure they wanted. And so, in a painfully time-consuming and expensive two-steps-forward-one-step-back kind of a way, these debates were played out in committee and we eventually got the agreement we needed to do the home-building everyone wanted. That is the price we pay for the pressure politicians are under to be seen to be doing something. If they hadn't gone about it this way, they would have missed out on a lot of visibility, and as far as many amongst the voting public were concerned, they may as well not have done anything at all. It's amazing what we could do, the saying goes, when no one cares who gets the credit. This is true, but politicians who don't care about getting the credit are the ones who don't get re-elected – because nobody knows what they stand for, or because they're boring, or because people think they don't do anything.

Another forum where local politicians work together is the Local Government Association, which represents councils across the country and the political spectrum. It regularly lobbies government on issues where members agree, and there are plenty of those, from housing to public health, education, public amenities, planning, and more. One perennial ambition of the LGA is simply to see councils granted more power, and for more local decision-making. Given the highly centralised nature of British (or at least English) politics, that's something most local politicians would sign up to in a heartbeat.

What about MPs, then? Back in September 2021, I was sitting at a fringe meeting venue chatting to an MP and a couple of staffers before the meeting started. Who's your MP? they asked me. I told them – it's Mid Derbyshire's Pauline Latham. "Ah, Pauline! She's great. We work with her all the time." They went on to tell me how many years she's been involved in international development and how much she has done to champion the cause. Great stuff. I was at the Labour Party Conference. Pauline Latham is a Conservative.

Is it unusual to hear praise heaped on an opposition politician in this way? I don't think so. Politicians of different parties work together all the time. There are massive areas of overlap. This doesn't extend to all policy areas, of course, and in fact Pauline Latham's view on international development funding is at odds with that of her government. She was one of the rebels voting against the 2021 cut to the foreign aid budget. But nationally and locally, the common ground between politicians is much greater than I expected before I was elected.

While there are those who would like to see us bickering less, that view is by no means universal. In my doorstep conversations I've spoken to those who wanted to see Keir Starmer back the government more, particularly as we came out of the pandemic. But just as many seem to say he isn't doing enough to oppose the government. When I let people know of the existence of the opposite set of views, they're quite surprised. In actual fact, he's doing both. Unlike Brighton and Hove, the government with its parliamentary majority doesn't need opposition support to get things through. But in terms of where Labour stands, sometimes they back government proposals and sometimes they don't. In an open multi-party system, it does fall to opposition parties to scrutinise whoever is in government and put forward alternatives. There are, after all, many ways of doing things and it's healthy for different ideas to be aired. The government also needs to be held to account in terms of its competence, and the behaviour of its representatives. An opposition which didn't do this would be remiss. But there will be times, and there were plenty of them during the pandemic, when government and opposition agree.

The problem is that the latter doesn't penetrate the news filter in the same way. People agreeing with each other just isn't very newsworthy. The voter not knowing Labour's position on Russia and Ukraine is just one example. When Labour opposes something, it's much more likely to be reported. When the opposition backs the government, it may get a passing mention, but a full-on PMQs' attack will get the lion's share of airtime and headlines. And so the impression is given, through selective coverage, that politicians do nothing but disagree.

The same principle applies with our own materials. If a leaflet only gets ten seconds, we can't waste it on listing all the areas where we agree with the other parties: we need to focus on how we're different, our areas of distinction, how things would be better under Labour. But why so negative? some ask. You don't have to dwell on all the bad stuff so much. I sometimes say the same when I'm involved in creating these materials: I'd much rather put out a leaflet full of positive ideas for the future instead of criticisms of the other side. The truth is, as I'm told on a regular basis, negative campaigning works. We are a political party with an objective of gaining power so that we can put our values into practice. This isn't easy, so we have to look at what seems to cut through with voters. If nobody wanted us to bicker, negative campaigning wouldn't work.

These contradictions occur partly because electors are different from each other. Some want upbeat and positive, others want (or respond to) a strong attack. Voters also differ enormously in terms of their focus: on the doorstep it's fascinating how some are tuned into issues in their local area, while others have absolutely no interest in that but are motivated entirely by the national narrative. In leaflets we have to decide which to go for, or gamely try and do all at once, having something to say to everyone, both in terms of subject matter and tone. The fact that the result only gets ten seconds is a bit of a pity really.

While agreement between parties is normal, so is disagreement within them. All political parties accommodate supporters with a range of views. Our first-past-the-post electoral system exacerbates this: smaller parties miss out and the two biggest parties have to court an incredibly broad voter base. But even without this, compromise is part of politics: such a vast range of opinion exists on all topics that in order to get anything done you have to come together with people you don't agree with about everything, and find common ground. However, diversity of views within a political party is something that's not readily accepted. Of course parties ultimately have to decide what their policies are and stick to them (see later for collective decision-making), but that's never going to erase difference and dissent entirely. We need differences. We need disagreements, in order to be able to resolve them into a coherent whole which will gain enough support from the country. We need discussion. We need debate. In short, we need to bicker.

The word itself speaks volumes. It suggests opposition for its own sake, meaningless argument over unimportant details, the different sides no better than each other. Instead of bickering we could talk about having different opinions, comparing experiences, reflecting a broad base of stakeholders. But terms like this are often dismissed as smoothing over, in an overwhelmingly negative political environment where any suggestion of disagreement is pounced upon with enthusiasm by commentators.

There's also something of a fascination with personality clashes. The BBC even made a whole series about the Blair versus Brown relationship. I didn't watch any of it. Frankly I don't care if they hated each other. The only thing that matters to me is whether we had effective government. If multiple arguments were had to get there, so be it. A cabinet or shadow cabinet should include people with different backgrounds who stand in different places under the Labour umbrella, just like our voters. Political differences are often strongly felt. We wouldn't all be doing this if we didn't have views or think that it mattered. Somehow we have to navigate all that. An expectation that we're never going to fall out is just unrealistic. Yet it's something that interviewers come back to again and again, making it about personalities and snubs and loyalty or lack thereof, in a way which presents it all like some eternal soap opera.

When they get fed up of bickering in the news, folk could switch over to the Parliament Channel. Here they would see bickering the dignified way (with the exception of the half-hourly-per-week PMQs): representatives giving well-researched speeches pulling proposals apart and commenting on the issues of the day, most of which never make it into a news bulletin. A chance to watch your elected representative while they go about doing their job, or part of it, anyway.

For those with less time, Radio 4's *Today in Parliament* has become a regular half hour in my listening. The first ten minutes generally covers subjects I've already heard on the news. The other twenty is where the sound bites are replaced with more considered speeches, news from the Lords where the tone is often very different, personal reflections, compliments across the house, and, quite often, humour. Theresa May recently had the entire Commons in stitches during a moving speech paying tribute to the Queen[xi]. All of this might not have the drama of a soap, but it's real life.

Locally, every council meeting at Brighton and Hove is webcast. Here you can start to see very clearly the areas of difference and overlap, where parties agree and where they do not, and why. Full Council is the most overtly political of these, with many of the 54 members standing up to deliver their speeches on the various notices of motion. Often we don't get onto these until ten o'clock at night, so the live audience might understandably be a bit thin on the ground, apart from the dogged local press, of course. Some of my colleagues dedicated an entire day to the writing of these speeches. Others scribbled theirs on a blank piece of paper during the pre-meet and the break –

particularly if they didn't have the option of taking a day off work. While some moments during these meetings weren't particularly dignified, on the whole the points were carefully thought out and researched, passionate and articulate, and it was certainly a good opportunity to find out what people really stood for. It's a shame that these notices of motion when passed generally resulted in nothing more than a letter being sent to the government, followed, some months later, by some anodyne ministerial response. And all of this in front of a tiny audience of electors. Still, in some ways it went to the absolute heart of what we mean by an open democracy.

One of the key benefits of democracy is that it enables us to manage differences of opinion without one side having to gain dominance some other way. Do we want to bicker, and win or lose an argument, or do we want to arm ourselves and fight for our views to be heard? Or do we want to live in a place where disagreement isn't allowed at all? Political debate may be irritating at times, but it's better than pitchforks. Or guns. Being on the losing side of a vote is galling, but at least you can walk away afterwards. Politicians have the freedom to agree or disagree with each other as they see fit, to work together or to oppose, based on their values, on their assessment of the situation, on their understanding of public opinion. In my experience they make full use of this freedom. Do we really want it any other way?

Tracey Hill

5. They're Boring

In a world that has so much to entertain us, politics doesn't always succeed, let's say, in grabbing the attention of the electorate. Local government even less so. It's all about dog poo and potholes, isn't it? Actually, it's about whatever people want it to be about in their local area. What's the issue people raise with you most often? a former Labour activist asked me once. Parking, I told him. He seemed disappointed. But those who do engage set the agenda for the rest, and it's an agenda that doesn't seem to appeal to a lot of people.

It doesn't have to be that way: local authorities deal with some pretty fundamental things. We saw that during the pandemic. Councils were responsible for moving rough sleepers off the streets and putting them up in hotels, cooking and distributing meals in the community, handing out grant funding to affected businesses, closing down parks and play areas, preparing retail spaces for opening up safely, dealing with people moving out of hospital into social care, buying and distributing PPE, and more. During those critical times, officers were moved into urgent roles as services were turned upside down to provide what was needed. In the meantime – and this may be different for other councillors – my inbox went strangely quiet. Casework and the usual resident queries fell away, and when they started to come back again it was to ask things like when they were going to start cutting the grass again.

The issues local councillors talk about are those raised most often by residents, and these tend to be around the services that are highly visible and that everyone has some experience of. Even so, quite a lot of people don't seem that interested in, or even aware of, the day-to-day stuff – unless something has gone wrong.

The bins getting collected every week is boring. The bins not getting collected – that's a bit more interesting. When we have a bin strike and massive pile-ups of refuse in every neighbourhood, that's really interesting. Smelly, but interesting. A service redesign that goes wrong, resulting in long queues and delays, is interesting. A project that runs out of money and has to be abandoned is interesting. A heart-rending series of miscommunications resulting in the failure to protect a child attracts huge attention. At the same time, the names of vastly more children go ever unspoken, the children who were identified as at risk and were adequately safeguarded, and went on to lead normal lives. Like the project that completes successfully and ahead of time and the service redesign that progresses without hitch, they pass below the radar.

Of course the media focuses on the bad news. Generally speaking, news is bad news. But where do we balance this against all the good stuff? In a world where to get more than ten seconds of head space politics has to try to compete as another form of entertainment, we don't. Tabloids and social media love the double yellow lines that were painted around a parked car or over the top of a dead cat, never mind that thousands of miles of road are maintained perfectly sensibly. The Handforth Parish Council meeting in which the proper authority was recognised and business done with general agreement didn't go viral. The disaster, exceptional though it may be, becomes the only thing that gets airplay. No wonder, then, that the impression people end up with is that politics is just one disaster after another. This applies even more nationally. Competence is boring, or just taken for granted. Which is odd, as politicians are also accused of incompetence a lot of the time (see "They're Incompetent"). Even so, competence in itself doesn't seem to be enough. Politicians are expected to generate interest, spark, charisma – to entertain as well as get the job done.

Charisma and local politics rarely go hand in hand. When I was serving, I developed an ability to talk at great length about pavement parking, LED street lamps and community composting, explain exactly why it was that you couldn't recycle a Tetrapak, and describe how you went about requesting a dropped kerb. I was a veritable walking encyclopaedia of planning applications in my local area and their entire history, which I would delightedly share with anyone I happened to be with while passing one of them by. When visiting other towns, I photographed the signage on the bins and compared the real-time bus displays to the ones back home. And I know I'm not alone.

Fortunately, the expectation isn't as great at local level, where politics is an ensemble game and each councillor just one player. You don't have to rush towards the limelight at all times: there's some scope to do the job how you want to do it. Some councillors make rousing speeches in meetings, others don't but are energetic in their local communities, or determined in their pursuance of casework. Getting elected locally doesn't make you famous: councillors, sometimes even council leaders, often enjoy low levels of public recognition.

At the other end of the political spectrum is the person constantly held in the harsh and unforgiving glare of the public eye – the leader of the party. I admit I'm mystified as to why so many people on the doorstep seem so obsessed with the personal characteristics of this one individual, when there are so many other things that also matter. This is what I hear: "Well...I don't know about [insert name of every Labour leader we've had since I started door-knocking (except Corbyn – voters' issues with him were of a different order)]. He's just – he doesn't have that...there's just nothing about him." Am I wrong to be frustrated that so many voting decisions seem to hinge exclusively on one politician's personal qualities, despite the policies, despite anything I've done, despite anyone's record in government, nationally or locally?

Voters seem to be searching for some X factor that can't be defined or described. For me, if someone has achieved a lot in life and exhibits the key skills that a politician needs – is articulate, empathetic, bridge-building and understanding (of information and people) – that's charisma enough. Folk I speak to on the doorstep seem to want more. As I said, competence is boring. But isn't boring what we want, if it means that the business of government will go according to plan and services delivered without mishap?

Election turnout is generally on the decline in most democracies in the world. In the UK, turnout for upper-level local elections is around 35% compared with around 67% for general elections[xii]. For parish and town council elections, turnouts of 20% are not unusual. It is ironic that local elections have lower turnouts but local politicians are more trusted by the electorate. Perhaps those two things are linked, if the very act of choosing politicians heaps expectation upon them which they then don't meet. This doesn't bode well for the future of democracy, and suggests a destiny in which we fall ever more out of love with our elected representatives.

What can be done? Some believe that it's down to politicians to generate more enthusiasm for politics by being a bit more exciting. But is it, entirely? Shouldn't it be enough to be good at the job? Should people expect to be entertained as well as served by the people they elect? Isn't that demanding too much? More worryingly, isn't it going to end up rewarding charisma at the expense of competence?

The responsibility seems to lie entirely with a party's leadership, not just for how engaged voters are, but also how knowledgeable. I don't know what Starmer stands for, someone said to me at around the time Russia was poised to invade Ukraine. She didn't know what Keir Starmer's position was on Ukraine, and felt that she should. Have you Googled it? I asked. Three words should get you there – *Keir Starmer Ukraine*, for example (it did – I tried it later). This was pugnacious, but I was curious enough to risk annoying someone. Her answer was along the lines that she didn't see why she should. She felt that Keir Starmer and the Labour Party were entirely responsible for what was inside her head about them. In some ways I get this. There is a communication job to do. But is it completely one-sided? Is there no onus at all on the citizens of a democracy to find out what they feel they need to know? I guess not, but this does leave politicians doing all the running.

When I Googled *Keir Starmer Ukraine*, it was pretty clear what his position was within the snippets of the top ten results without having to click any further. There were references to opinion pieces in at least two national dailies and links to TV interviews. So he and the party put some effort into getting it out there. But it didn't crop up in news headlines, it wouldn't have featured in two-minute news roundups, it wasn't on the main evening news, it probably wasn't on a front page anywhere. For it to qualify for that, Starmer would have had to be saying something markedly different from the government, and although his position was distinct, it wasn't completely opposite; it was broadly the same (see "They're Always Bickering").

While I was doing this, I also thought I'd use Google Trends to see how many people had actually searched for this term. Not very many, was the answer: fair enough. I then looked at what the top five searches had been on that day. They were: *bbc, news, google, weather*, and *bbc news*. In fact those are the top five most of the time. What this tells me, apart from that a lot of people use Google to search for Google, is that millions of people out there are consistently pretty interested in the news. This is heartening. But it also demonstrates the huge influence of news editors. Where people have a tool at their fingertips that they could use to search for anything at all, they voluntarily limit themselves to what other people think are the newsworthy topics. They're happy for someone else to tell them what's news and what isn't. This gives news editors a huge amount of influence over public opinion.

I go along with this in that I, too, want to know what's in the news. I want to know what people are talking about, even if it's decided by a frighteningly small number of people. But the news filter is immensely powerful. Politics filtered through the news only ever shows the short term, and usually only the bad bits, the mess-ups and the blunders, one pratfall after another. It's like trying to understand human life through one never-ending episode of *You've Been Framed!*

And what should politicians do to fix it? This is problematic. What can politicians say to people who have been on the receiving end of a narrative that's almost entirely negative for so long that they are no longer prepared to believe anything positive? All I can think of is to keep doing what my colleagues and I are doing – knock on some more doors, ask people what they think, be open and honest, try to have a conversation. The idea that we should try and entertain as well fills me with dread, and, if it leads to ever greater promises being made, it will only enhance expectations further and cause greater disappointment later.

What's the best we can hope for, or the worst we should fear? My hope is that the desire to retain our democratic system goes wider than just politicians. We need to find ways of celebrating democracy and demonstrating the benefits it has brought us. My fear is that it is already too late, that the positives simply won't be believed, that we are already in an era where someone with sufficient charisma could offer an alternative which is perceived to be better than anything people could choose for themselves.

We're Not All the Same

6. They Lie

The lying politician is an absolute classic trope. You can't believe a word any politician says, right? It's clear that a widespread perception that politicians everywhere are incapable of telling the truth is going to severely impact on trust and engagement with politics. So where does this belief come from and how accurate is it? I suggest below that there are four different ways in which politicians are seen to lie. Let's look at each in turn.

Statistics

To go back to the 200 homes we delivered in Brighton and Hove, after much discussion and examination of spreadsheets, our housing leaflet of December 2018 actually said this:

We provided almost 200 new council homes, more than previous administrations and many other councils.

We also included this key footnote: "New council homes provided, bought or on site since May 2015".

If we'd only included the homes that were fully completed, or only the number we'd built ourselves rather than buy-backs (a new policy that wasn't in our manifesto) we wouldn't have got to 200. On the other hand, we could have included those that had planning permission but where building work hadn't actually started. We could possibly have found a way to include the joint venture, also not in our manifesto, and it was suggested that we were within our rights to include pitches on traveller sites that had come into being on our watch. We didn't. So the number we claimed could have been higher than 200, or it could have been lower, depending on what we thought we could legitimately count.

Was it more than previous administrations and other councils? Definitely, though this annoyed the Greens, who argued that they set up the pipeline that enabled us to do it. This is true, though creating a pipeline is infinitely easier than getting the homes actually built, and the hindrances we faced would also have been there for any other administration. Besides, all incoming administrations inherit the work of their predecessors. Realistically, it takes longer than four years to do anything on any scale, so this kind of thing is bound to happen in places where power changes hands on a regular basis.

Our 200 claim was perfectly legitimate, but had the opposition chosen to challenge them, we could all have had an almighty spat about numbers, something that can be off-putting for voters. Some might conclude that "you can say anything with statistics" and reject all the data entirely. This is a pity, because statistics are a far more objective way of seeing the world than alternatives such as anecdote and personal experiences, which are inevitably limited.

Information can be used in different ways to support different interpretations of situations and events. But there are right ways of doing this, and wrong ways. The UK Statistics Authority (UKSA) has a wealth of guidelines and a code of conduct, in order to promote the proper use of stats and maintain public confidence in official data[xiii]. When things go awry, they can step in. A recent Home Office claim, repeated by then Prime Minister Boris Johnson, that the crime rate had fallen by 14% between 2019 and 2021 prompted an investigation[xiv]. It turned out that this comparison excluded crimes classified as fraud and computer misuse. If they were included, the crime rate would be up by 14%, not down. The watchdog described the claim as misleading, since the exclusion was not consistently mentioned and there was no particular justification for it. This claim, therefore, was wrong, and, basically, a lie. Other claims, however, are perfectly legitimate. The Home Office, other government departments, and councils everywhere produce a steady stream of numerically-based press releases without prompting any investigation.

While it's understandable to want to walk away from all statistics out of a feeling that it's impossible to get to the bottom of them, it's also overly dismissive. In a democracy where in order to win political power you have to demonstrate certain qualities, including effectiveness, it's inevitable – and right – that those who are vying for voters' support make use of data to demonstrate their points. Ultimately it's down to voters to exercise some judgement in terms of interpreting it all. Politicians should of course avoid using statistics in a downright inaccurate and misleading way, and it's right that they're called out when they do. But if the general conclusion whenever this happens is that all statistics are a lie, this will severely limit the public's understanding of what kind of state things are in, what the true causes are of our various problems, and what will work to address them.

I also feel that it's unhelpful of commentators, and sometimes politicians themselves, to start shouting "It's a lie!" whenever they come across an argument they don't agree with. A wrong opinion is not a lie. The very existence of different opinions, infuriating though some of them are, is evidence that there's debate and challenge, and that's a good thing. Life in parts of the world where only one version of the truth is allowed may be simpler, but simplicity has its drawbacks.

"I didn't know anything about it."

There's also the personal sort of lying. What did a particular person know about a particular incident prior to it going belly-up? Did they go to a party, or didn't they? Politicians are rightly expected to have higher standards given the position of power they hold. It's bad news for all politicians when someone with a high profile is caught out in some self-protecting lie. However much you might remind voters that just because someone on the front benches did something unjustifiable doesn't mean that your local councillor has, somehow the mud seems to stick everywhere. As observed earlier, an instance of poor behaviour is assumed by commentators, and much of the public at large, to be typical of how all politicians behave, as opposed to the exception.

How to resolve this? Well, it would be great if certain politicians could stop lying themselves into a cocked hat in the first place. I'm sure we can all agree on that. Until that day comes, perhaps the delight with which negative news is pounced on by the media could sometimes be tempered with a willingness to present some positives as well. Do we hear much about some of the great things that politicians do, in terms of their personal behaviour? Going the extra mile for their constituents, or being particularly compassionate or understanding about something, maybe? It definitely happens.

I can almost hear a sharp intake of breath at this idea, as if it would be the thin end of the wedge, and before we know it we'll be Belarus. But are we sure about that? Is what we're doing now really so great? Commentators who present all politicians equally negatively are doing democracy no favours at all. I've even spoken to voters so fed up with it all that they don't seem to care if someone is caught breaking the rules, particularly if it's someone they like. They're all at it anyway, right? So what the heck? And he's a nice chap. If likeability becomes more important than sticking to the rules, that could open the gates to someone who charms the electorate so much that they can do whatever they want. I absolutely think this could happen: it may be that there's more than one road to Belarus.

One time we are nice about politicians is after they have passed away. Tributes to the murdered politicians Jo Cox and David Amess were warm and moving, and came from all sides of the political spectrum. The same happens when politicians, nationally and locally, die of natural causes while in office. How might voters respond if they heard more of this mutual respect in the normal course of things, as opposed to only in the aftermath of loss or even more horrific events? It would need to filter through the media, though, and this may be the real problem: while politicians in Parliament and the council chamber regularly give kudos to each other, this rarely translates into front-page news. How differently might we feel about politics if it did?

"That's terrible. I'll go away and fix it."

What about personal integrity? Do politicians really care, or is it all an act? One regular complaint from residents is that they told their representative about some issue, and the politician in question seemed sympathetic and promised to get back to them, but never did. This is understandably irritating, and does nothing for anyone's reputation. I know politicians who are scrupulous about ensuring they get back to people, whether it's with good news or not so good. Others less so, though they were probably well-intentioned. Residents may often not be aware of just how busy an MP's office is, or the inbox of a councillor who is doing the job part time. If not, it really is incumbent on the MP or councillor in question to give people some idea of how long it might take for their query to be dealt with, and also to be realistic about what the response might be.

There have been times when residents have raised something, often with some passion, that just aren't going to be taken up, because they can't be sufficiently prioritised or because there just isn't enough of a reason to. At one door I knocked on, a woman ushered me through her house into the back garden to show me the thing she was so outraged about. It turned out that her neighbour at the back had built a garden shed very close to her back fence. It wasn't a big shed. It didn't have windows. The back fence was some distance from the house. I couldn't share her outrage. It wasn't doing any harm, as far as I could see. I can understand how some councillors in my shoes might have offered to look into the planning regulations, for example, or advised her to lodge an enforcement complaint. For my part, I fear I left her somewhat deflated, but better that than go away with an empty promise. There is pressure on elected representatives to try and make everybody happy all the time, but we simply cannot. If this is what citizens are expecting, it may well explain why so many are so disappointed. Politicians should be taking these opportunities to be realistic with the public about how things work – but not everyone will welcome this.

There are also the issues that are important but hard to address, such as the bus fares and traffic calming examples from before. What we can and can't do isn't necessarily straightforward. We could make all bus fares free, for example. Perfectly possible: Labour made museums free. But it would be something for national government, and would obviously cost a lot. While we might not be able to sort it simply by putting a line in a budget somewhere, we can register bus fares as a concern and work towards it in the longer term, nationally or locally. However, I fear that on the ground this is considered the same as not doing anything at all. Perhaps more can be done to persuade people that sharing their thoughts makes a difference, even if it might not be evident until years down the line.

"I'm telling you honestly what I think."

What about lying in terms of personal opinions? Integrity is important. But I want to spend a bit of time considering the matter of collective decision-making.

As discussed, it's inevitable that people of the same party sometimes have different views. But if you're part of a political group of councillors, you need to agree a group position and stick to it. This ought to be done through discussion. Bearing in mind the sheer volume of business going through at any one time, not all decisions can be debated. Mostly, the shared values of the party we all belong to will be enough – after all, we got elected on a manifesto and we knew what was in it. But there will be particular issues where there's disagreement – in my time examples were transport (bike lanes) and development (whether or not to allocate certain sites for housing). Once the matter has been debated and decided, by vote if necessary, it's accepted that everyone gets behind the decision whether they supported it or not. That means that sometimes councillors will be expected to publicly support a position they themselves didn't agree with – because they are part of a group which made that decision.

Doesn't that result in people lying? Strictly speaking, I guess so. When people are telling you what they think, it might sometimes be the position of the group, not what they personally think: they must back the group decision above their own. They should be prepared to do this: adherence to the group whip is something Labour candidates sign up to in advance.

Some parties, in particular the Greens, make a point of saying that they don't have a group whip and therefore you can trust all their representatives to tell you what they really think. At least, they say that in places where they're not in power. When they are in power, or close to it, it seems to me that the unanimity of their decision-making is exactly the same as it is with the other parties. When the Greens first led the council in Brighton and Hove, splits and divisions caused a lot of difficulties and generated a shed load of bad publicity, but in the time that I've served they're no more "divided" than anyone else. Truth is, it's the only practical way of going about things if you want to get anything done. In general, the claims of smaller parties that they will sweep away the old order and do things completely differently will usually result in disappointment: all parties and politicians are operating under the same constraints and in the shadow of the same expectations.

The collective decision principle applies just as much to a board of directors of a company, or trustees of a charity, or a school governing body. It achieves nothing to express disagreement with a collective decision after the event. It will undermine the authority of that body, not just in respect of the current issue but all others as well. The rebel may feel better about themselves, but that isn't going to get them or anyone else very far. There are multiple other situations in our economic and social lives where the decision of the group trumps the view of the individual. So calling it lying is pretty reductionist. A party politician, like anyone who operates as part of a bigger group, is there to support the ambitions and aims of the party above their own. It's the party that gets things done, not the politician.

Of course there are exceptions, particular circumstances in which someone will go their own way. I have. There have to be red lines, things that can't be overlooked, otherwise there's insufficient accountability internally. But as a general rule toeing the line is part of the job of being a politician. Which is not, first and foremost, feeling good about yourself, but making real change happen in society at large.

The concept of the whip is perhaps talked up a little in the media. The archaic name doesn't help – it conjures up all kinds of unhelpful images. Locally, the job of the chief whip is to organise the political group and make sure it functions properly. In my experience the whips were people-managers, trouble-shooters, communicators, advice-givers. Those elements were more important than discipline. Things may be different in Parliament, but it seems to me that backbenchers quite often make speeches that critique their own government – and quite often rebel. Parliament is different, though: we're talking much bigger numbers – hundreds of MPs (a minimum of 326 for a parliamentary majority) versus a local administration of perhaps twenty to thirty councillors.

So, do politicians lie? Some do, but not all of them, and it doesn't happen as often as is generally perceived. But I wonder if this is really the point. Even if we remain strictly within the truth, or at least the justifiable, are we promising too much with our rhetoric? Are we suggesting we can solve problems more quickly and easily than is realistic? Are we making out that we can please everybody when that's largely impossible? If so, we should desist and start telling it straight. But we do need an electorate which is happy to hear it that way.

7. They Don't Answer the Question

We're Not All the Same

Early on in my days as a Labour member, fired up with enthusiasm, I went to a meeting featuring the then Health Secretary Alan Johnson. He explained in his own way, to a fairly friendly audience, some of Labour's policies and actions. He spoke about how the NHS had been formed, and that at the heart of it, particularly concerning GPs and others who opposed it, was compromise. Many of the initiatives taken by the Labour government were also compromises, he said, and addressed some of these in detail. This was a revelation to me – not in terms of what he said, but the fact that if you let a seasoned politician talk about something they know a lot about, they can actually be quite interesting.

The leaflet-scruncher mentioned earlier perhaps demonstrated the more common view that exposure to unfettered politician, either verbally or in written form, is both unpleasant and dangerous. Had Johnson been interviewed instead of having free rein to speak – as he often was while in post, of course – the conversation would have been pinned down to whatever the interviewer wanted to focus on. Attempts to provide context or bring in other considerations might have been treated as avoidance or dodging the question. While sometimes this focus is essential to hold politicians to account, if that's all voters ever get, I think they're missing out.

A piece on the Today programme in February 2022 discussed the demise of the 5 p.m. COVID briefings; a commentator compared these briefings to Belarussian state-controlled television, where dictators sit for hours in front of a camera speechifying about how great things are. While journalistic challenge is of course good, this seemed a slight exaggeration. To state the obvious, our politicians aren't dictators: they were elected. Is it really the case that allowing them to address the electorate in their own words for a few minutes at a time will tip us into tyranny?

I spoke to a guy on the doorstep one evening. Any issues? The buses, he said, were too expensive. And there was speeding traffic in the street. Speed bumps would help. The bus fares are set by the bus company, I explained: the council doesn't have a role in that. And I could ask about speed bumps but they're a common request and very expensive. So, he said: You can't reduce the bus fares and you can't put in speed bumps. Is that what you're saying?

The quick answer to his question was yes. In the short term the council couldn't have delivered either of these. I couldn't just trot off and have a word with a couple of people, make it all happen in a month or two. But with a bit more time, I could have said that it didn't mean nothing could be done. While the council can't dictate bus fares, for millions of people right now, buses are entirely free. This is on the back of national legislation and relies on finding the money elsewhere, but it can be done. Over time buses can be more affordable, and technology helps – contactless payment, through ticketing and so on. And it's useful to hear from residents that it's something they want, as councillors can keep raising the issue, with the bus company, within the party to shape future policy, or elsewhere.

As for traffic calming, the council receives so many requests that it has a methodology for dealing with them. Someone does an initial inspection and decides (based on defined criteria, such as how busy the street is, how many people are trying to cross, who is trying to cross, etc.) if it's high enough priority. Most aren't. Those that are go onto a list which is published on the website. There are roughly 40 sites on the list. But the council only has the money to address a handful every year, maybe half a dozen. So even if you get on the list it can be a long wait to get to the top. At which point there'll be a consultation and we get to hear from all the people who aren't so keen on the idea. But every year the handful of schemes that do go ahead make the road system just that little bit safer and casualties are generally on the decline. I could also have mentioned to him that anything involving alterations on the highway is enormously expensive and mired in regulation. There may be other ways to discourage speeding – by using signage, for example, or running local campaigns, or setting up a Community Speedwatch group. And in the meantime other things lead to more excess deaths than road accidents: poor air quality and cold homes, for example. Focusing resources into the thing that's most top-of-mind might not be the best way. (I have a theory that the issues people raise on the doorstep are more likely to be the things that actually fall within their line of sight while being asked the question.)

There was so much more I could have said to him besides yes or no, and this is stuff that I've learned myself over time, either from responses to previous queries or from briefing meetings or committee reports: time spent by me, paid for by taxpayers, so that I can bring the council to the people, as well as vice versa. To me it's not waffle or changing the subject: it's the very heart of the matter, the actual reasons, in real life, why things that seem such a good idea don't just happen. Simply answering with yes or no does nothing to illuminate things where, in a changing landscape there are multiple possibilities, multiple stakeholders, multiple barriers and competing priorities.

Challenge is good. Challenging media interviews should involve asking politicians difficult questions. But the questions themselves aren't always that helpful. At its best, a challenging interview gets right to the crux of an issue and strips away all the obfuscation to put the person responsible inescapably on the spot. At its worst, it's like a Punch and Judy show where the subject is bashed on the head over and over again with the same unanswerable question, for no particular broader benefit. Often a question is being asked in a certain way to generate headlines, to entrap the subject into doing something like contradict a party policy or undermine someone else, rather than genuinely address an important topic.

Listening to such interviews, even those with representatives of the current government with whom I fundamentally disagree, I find myself frustrated when they're cut off before they get to the end of what they were saying, often by a question which is a version of something that's already been asked. What was the "on the other hand" that we never got to? What was the second of the two points they wanted to make? We never get to hear it and are forced down another path entirely based on the agenda of the interviewer. I'm not saying this because I think I'll agree with the politician's answers, but they are making decisions on the basis of briefings, information, consultation and negotiation, and I wouldn't mind hearing a full explanation. Do we really need to be protected in this way from hearing directly from the people who represent us? If so, who exactly is doing the protecting and what are they getting out of it? Can we not judge for ourselves whether a politician has answered the question or not, or at any rate told us something worth knowing?

There are opportunities for politicians to go into more detail, for example written opinion pieces, or even books and podcasts. There's also the Parliament Channel where you can watch entire parliamentary debates, Select Committee sessions and a ton of other business. Many of these have small audiences, however. Locally, the political group leaders submitted regular columns in the local press, and media coverage of what the council did was, actually, quite thorough. On top of all that, we made a constant effort to try and get across to the voting public what it was that we were doing, and why – and to answer their questions.

One important means of doing this was leaflets. We'd spend hours honing every word. Actually the main thing we were doing was reducing the word count to an absolute minimum. People will spend ten seconds reading it, they say. Not much more than a short pause on the item's journey from letterbox to recycling bin. Use it wisely. Some pieces of literature don't even enjoy that: the scrunched-up leaflet earlier couldn't even have been inside the house for more than ten seconds. On my leafleting rounds, it's not uncommon for people to refuse a leaflet altogether, sometimes with an air that suggests they might catch something nasty if they spent any time looking at it. No thanks – I'm a Tory, some might explain. You can still read it, I say. Me, I always read the Tory leaflets. But it isn't just that. There's an assumption that the things are full of propaganda and in some way harmful, although many with this view might happily suck up our luridly opinionated national press commentary on a regular basis.

The ten-second rule is why in our leaflets we have to simplify enormously. We have to focus on where we differ in our views and approach from other parties. We can't justify the space to make some convoluted point about how we agree with part of something but not all of it. We can't talk about short term versus long term, or decisions made on a balance of considerations, like Alan Johnson did at that meeting. Not enough space, not enough time. So the result comes out black and white. On the doorstep, though, there is time for this, to explain how we came to arrive at our position, to offer something much more nuanced and contextualised. That's why these conversations are so valuable – when they happen.

I'm offering no guarantees about the quality of politicians' responses: not everyone is Alan Johnson and

I've heard my fair share of meaningless waffle over the years. There are certainly times when challenge is needed to highlight when a difficult matter is being avoided. But I sometimes feel that communicating with the electorate is like trying to perform some kind of mental keyhole surgery, squeezing complexity and history and cost benefit balances into the tiny amounts of time that people are prepared to listen for, their reluctance stemming from the view perpetuated in our political discourse that nothing coming out of a politician's mouth can be trusted. Not every issue can accurately be explained by answering yes or no to a series of loaded questions or summarised in a hundred words. If we want people to properly understand what the real issues are so that they can judge for themselves and make informed decisions, we need a more meaningful dialogue than that. Before it could happen, though, some of the blanket negativity, which so limits politicians' opportunities to communicate in any depth, would have to be stripped away.

8. They Don't Listen

The rule of thumb, as mentioned earlier, is that a leaflet through the door enjoys ten seconds of attention before going straight into the recycling box. After all our agonised deliberations over every word of the text, efforts to line up suitable and permissioned photos, and begging phone calls to members to get them pushed through letterboxes by the thousand, it always felt as though something should happen as a result. Our lovingly executed propaganda, which we'd have to fundraise to afford, should surely change everything, set the world on fire. Generally, there wasn't much response at all. Unless, of course, it contained something about parking.

In my neck of the woods, parking was a subject everyone had a view on. Shortly after my colleagues and I were elected in 2015, a residents' parking zone came into operation in Fiveways, an area adjoining the Hollingdean part of our ward. Practically overnight the streets of Hollingdean filled up with cars, transits, minibuses and ice cream vans that never seemed to move. There were complaints. Some said they didn't go out any more for fear of losing their parking space. One resident, returning late one night from a family visit to Surrey, told us he got so fed up looking for a space that he drove all the way back to Surrey.

It didn't take long before people in those streets were calling for permit parking. However, we knew that plenty of others were dead set against the idea. We decided to hold a public meeting to gauge the strength of views across the neighbourhood. People came in large number, forming a long queue to get in. We were used to holding surgeries in that very room where one or two people, or more often nobody at all, showed up. But for parking, we ran out of chairs. People stood, leaned on the wall or perched on up-ended tables. We became concerned about fire regulations. Still they came.

Folk were angry. In areas where the parking was bad, they were angry they couldn't park anymore. In areas where the parking was okay, they were angry at the idea of having to pay to do exactly what they were already doing for nothing. Both perspectives were completely understandable. But despite the utterly divergent and very strongly held views, everyone was united about one thing, with heads nodding across the room every time it was articulated: it was all the fault of the council.

In a sense this is true because the problem was triggered by another permit zone coming into force. But that scheme was only set up because a majority of residents voted for it. The council was to blame, some said, for implementing a parking zone in the first place, somewhere in the city centre. And so they did – but only because residents there were begging them to. Inevitably, it pushed the problem outward with more and more requests for schemes.

In some ways CPZs provided a means of giving people exactly what they were asking for. A CPZ could stop oversized vans parking in their road, mystery vehicles parked in the same place for weeks at a time, and students in six-room shared houses all bringing their cars to the city during term times. Complaints about these things were frequent. A CPZ could fix them. And there was always a consultation and a vote before a scheme came in. This didn't impress those who were against. Permits were being foisted on neighbourhoods without the support of residents, they said: the council was doing it for the money.

The same argument had played itself out across the city numerous times. In April 2014, the local press reported on an upcoming consultation in an area known as the Triangle[xv]. Here are some of the online comments:

"It will happen anyway this is not a democracy anymore"

"Consultation my arse they are just going through the motion's as usual then whether people want it or not they will bring it in"

"There is no point whatsoever in them holding a consultation as they have proved time and time again that they will just ignore the results if they show that the public are against a proposal they put forward."

"We all know what consultation means. One of our councillors has already stated privately that this is going to happen anyway. The last area to go residents parking was the Roundhill area and a friend of mine who lives in that area states that not one person he has spoken to voted for it."

The committee report from the 2014 Triangle consultation is still online[xvi]. Of the residents who responded, 61% were in favour and 39% against. In

Round Hill back in 2012, despite the friend reporting that no one was in favour, 56% supported a scheme and 44% were against. Commentators like those above might claim that something was amiss with these results – some kind of back-office fudge to justify the council slipping its hands into residents' pockets. But the reporting is thorough and it's all online. In Hollingdean the support for permit parking was real: it was the reason why we'd called the meeting in the first place.

The issue came up repeatedly on the doorstep. Everyone in this street wants residents' parking, someone would say. A few doors down on the same road: "Permits? No one in this street wants them!" On this, and on other divisive topics, the breadth of public opinion is underestimated. Each side expects their elected representatives to agree with them. Politicians are thus trying to be on both sides of an argument at the same time. Sometimes that's possible by finding some common ground. Sometimes it just isn't. Whoever doesn't get their way could be tempted to accuse those in charge of not listening. In our case, after three thousand letters, a public meeting and numerous follow-up emails and petitions, I don't feel that any more listening was even possible. But whatever the council did or didn't do, some would be left displeased.

When my colleagues and I were first elected, quite a few people got in touch with issues that they'd raised before with previous incumbents. They wanted to try again with the new people. Fair enough – a new perspective might sometimes do the trick. I'd usually ask them what was said or done about the problem last time around. Nothing, was often the resident's answer. They did nothing. They said nothing. They weren't interested. They didn't listen. On further enquiry, I'd find out that quite a lot was said, or done, but not to the entire satisfaction of the resident.

I've come to believe that "They didn't listen" actually means something more like "They didn't do exactly what I wanted them to do". Unfortunately, expectations of what we could do were often too high. Sometimes what was being requested simply didn't fall within the powers of the local council, or wasn't going to benefit enough people to be prioritised when resources were already fully allocated. We were ready to suggest alternatives but people weren't always that impressed with them. None of this was due to a lack of listening. Even if we couldn't help in the short term, this kind of casework often informed longer term objectives – such as building new council homes – or got passed further up to central government or the party nationally for policy generation. A cynic would say that's just lip service and nothing comes of it, but I disagree. It just takes a long time, and the expectation is that everyone's problems are fixable at speed. If they're not, there's an assumption that it's because someone somewhere doesn't want them to be fixed.

There's not listening, and there's the specific not-listening felt by particular communities or demographics. I went to a meeting about the 50 bus that serves Hollingdean. The 50 is a terrible service, everyone agreed

– the worst in the city. No one cares about the 50. They have the oldest buses, the ones that have been phased out everywhere else. Whenever there's a problem it's the 50 that's taken off first. It's utterly unreliable. The drivers hate working the 50 route. Everyone knows this. A few months later I went to a meeting about the 24 bus that serves Coldean. The 24 is a terrible service. Old buses, unreliable, the first one that's taken off, the drivers hate it. The worst in the city. No one cares about the 24. Everyone knows this. On a similar vein, grass cutting is neglected in the outer areas: all the resources go into the city centre. Or into Brighton, not Hove. Or into Hove, not Brighton. Let's not even mention Portslade. In the Hollingdean Dip, people say that Fiveways is favoured in terms of street cleaning. In the Hollingdean Estate, people say that the Dip is favoured. They get anything they want up there, a man in Stanmer Park Road said. He meant the residents of Hollingbury Park Avenue, the next street along from his.

It's easy for people to believe that they're losing out, being overlooked, not being listened to, while the time, money and attention is going elsewhere. Pointing out evidence to the contrary doesn't seem to help. "There's nothing round here for kids," a man said to me, standing on his doorstep in East Brighton.

"What about that?" I asked, pointing behind me to a playground that was clearly visible from where he stood, over my left shoulder.

"Oh, that! Nah. I meant in the centre of Brighton. Nothing for kids. It's terrible." I might have stood there for some time listing all the things for kids in the centre of Brighton, but I'm not sure it would have made any difference. These sentiments are easily fed, and some people – often politicians – choose to feed them quite a lot.

Chatting to a councillor of another party about Coldean (of the 24 bus), he gave the view that there was nothing much there for local people. The neighbourhood was on the edge of the city, out of sight, forgotten. Really? I said. There's a library. That's more than Hollingdean has. True, he said. I went on. There's a doctor's surgery. A care home with a community cafe attached. Several shops, including a pharmacy. A pub, recently re-opened. More than one bus service. A church and church hall, both active in the community. Parks, play areas, allotments, open spaces. And the parking wasn't bad, generally speaking. He seemed surprised. Politicians don't generally say stuff like this. They're more likely to suggest that people are hard done by or missing out in some way. "You've never had it so good" has got to be one of the most famous political statements in British politics (though predictably enough, Harold MacMillan didn't actually say it[xvii]), but it's a sentiment that's unlikely to endear a politician to voters.

I'm not suggesting Coldean was the perfect place. The post office closed and there was no cashpoint anywhere. The buses could have been a lot better (they had a point about the 24), and the parking was getting worse. As local councillors we diligently helped sort out overgrown twittens, dodgy handrails, obstructive parking and noisy neighbours. We intervened with poorly maintained properties, missed bin collections and indifferently mowed grass. But to start all this by suggesting the area was some kind of wasteland would have been overly negative. I'm sure many residents would have gone along with the idea that Coldean was particularly overlooked. But the same idea would have been grasped at just as readily in Hollingdean, East Brighton and a dozen other places. Where this sentiment results in poor election turnout – "I'm not voting. What's the point? You never listen to us." – it's the saddest self-fulfilling prophecy in politics: it's difficult to listen to folk who are no longer saying anything.

I'm not claiming, either, that nobody loses out. Clearly, some do. Parts of my ward were pretty hard done by – polluted and over-developed with endless refuse and fly-tipping issues, drugs and antisocial behaviour. These areas had high numbers of rented properties, high churn, and low voter turnout. I got little in the way of casework from these streets. When we knocked no one was in – or no one answered – or residents had nothing in particular to say. And there were pockets like this all over, even in the more affluent areas. I know that within my ward children were going hungry, families were getting into debt and vulnerable adults were sitting alone in homes they couldn't afford to heat, but somehow in the course of my work I didn't often come face to face with this. I learned about them through officer reports and area-specific statistics, volunteers at food banks, the local primary school, the community centre. Working round the streets we tended to speak to the same people year after year, often about the same issues, but came back empty-handed from that block round the back of the garage where the buzzer never works, or the flats above the shops where the flyers on the doormat are always months old. It's been said that politicians have to campaign in poetry and govern in prose, but if we have to talk about bins and parking to establish ourselves amongst the voting public so that we can address social exclusion and support those who really need help, I'd say it was the other way round.

When voters choose to participate – whether at election time or otherwise – they can, and do, influence political decisions. To pick one example out of many, Brighton and Hove was installing on-street charging points for electric vehicles. Officers identified a stretch of street in Hollingdean suitable for four dedicated rapid charging spaces. The neighbours were consulted. They didn't like the idea. It was difficult enough to park already, they said, and besides, nobody has electric cars. The officers were set to drop it altogether, but my colleague and I got to hear about it. No one round there is going to get an electric car, we said, unless they have places to charge it up, and few residents had private driveways. We ended up with two spaces. I'd have preferred four. But to consult and then ignore the results of the consultation didn't seem right, so we compromised.

Nationally and locally, the electorate has enormous influence on political decisions and outcomes. To point to an obvious example: in June 2016, 75% of MPs voted to remain in the EU. We've now left the EU. The idea that politicians simply do what they want regardless of public opinion is a myth. Possibly a convenient one at times. It must be the fault of the politicians, mustn't it, if the world isn't how we would like it to be? But what if that weren't the case? What if things are the way they are because of the electorate? What if democracy does actually work the way it's intended, and people do have a say about things? It would mean that the voting public would need to accept some responsibility for the consequences of decisions they've made – and give themselves some credit, of course, when good news in politics is allowed.

There may even be times when things aren't how they should be because politicians are listening too much.

We're Not All the Same

9. They Have No Guts

Politicians are too worried about what people think of them. They cave in under public pressure. They turn whichever way the wind blows. They capitulate in the face of public opinion. They don't stand up for what's right. They have no principles. They have no guts.

Hang on a sec, though. I thought the problem was that they don't listen. Aren't they supposed to be trying to do what people want them to do? Isn't that the point of electing politicians in the first place?

In response to the city's chronic housing shortage, a major initiative came forward to provide low-rent homes. One proposed site was a council-owned plot of land in the urban fringe adjacent to Coldean. The plans were for a fairly intensive development of over 200 flats. There was some opposition, stemming from fears of negative impacts. While as part of the administration I supported the initiative in principle, I was all prepared to leave the vexed issue of planning permission to the Planning Committee, who are supposed to decide individual applications in an apolitical way. But then we had an election, roles changed, and I became the chair of the Planning Committee. When the proposal came up, I supported it, and it passed.

As expected, some residents were unhappy about this. I gave my reasons: we needed housing that local people could afford, the quality of the flats was perfectly acceptable, and urban fringe sites had to be included in our plan to meet our targets. The proposal included various biodiversity and public amenity elements, and the development was separate from Coldean itself, in a field surrounded by a thick bank of trees. It wouldn't have anything like the same impact as other developments which were progressing in other parts of the city. We needed the housing, and had to put it somewhere.

"I don't care about other parts of the city," said one resident, with something like pride. "I only care about Coldean."

Fair enough, you might say. Residents will be much more concerned about their own neighbourhoods. But what should a politician do when faced with this argument? According to the most vocal opponents of the scheme, because some Coldean residents objected to the proposals, I should have done the same. As a ward councillor, my job was to represent the people in my ward. But all councillors also have citywide responsibilities. We're tasked with making decisions in committee that impact on the city in its entirety. This dual role is something all politicians have, locally or nationally. MPs represent their constituency, but they also represent a government, or opposition, which has policies for the whole country. Residents might say that they only care about their immediate area, but councillors can't. For a councillor, "I don't care" doesn't work. If everyone thought like that we'd never get anything done. If the only consideration of councillors was to keep development out of their ward, we wouldn't build anything.

I made what I thought was the right decision for the ward and the city, despite the wishes and expectations of some of my constituents. This might be described as having guts. Needless to say, the residents didn't thank me for it. They accused me, in a multitude of different ways, of not listening. But there's a dichotomy here. This is how it seems to work: If voters are crying out for politicians to do something and they do it, they're listening. Unless it's a bad idea, in which case they have no guts. If their voters are crying out for them not to do something but they do it anyway, they're ignoring the electorate. Unless it's a good idea, in which case they're showing leadership. All eventualities are therefore covered, though whether something is a good idea or not is clearly highly subjective. One person's respect of democracy is another's pandering to the masses. One person's courageous leadership is another's contempt of public opinion.

Here it is in diagrammatic form:

IS IT POPULAR?			
	YES	Respecting democracy/ pandering to populism	No-brainer
	NO	Forget it	Showing leadership/ ignoring the electorate
		NO	YES

IS IT A GOOD IDEA?

But can a popular idea ever be bad? The voter is always right, aren't they? Who am I to disagree with my residents? Many see the role of politicians as simply to deliver whatever the electorate wants, but this isn't really workable. Democracy is about how we make collective decisions about big things that impact a lot of people all at once. Politicians can't personalise the world to fit the desires of each of their electors. We can't provide a one-to-one service. A single decision often results in winners and losers, if only perceptually. Besides, voters often disagree vehemently with each other. Both sides can never be happy if they're diametrically opposed.

We're Not All the Same

This probably sounds very patronising. We know what we want, I can hear people saying. Maybe so, but that doesn't necessarily make it deliverable or affordable. And what makes me think I know best? Well, it's largely because I've spent hours and hours in meetings and workshops, asking questions and reading reports.

In the Coldean example above, this included: the city's acute housing crisis; the high rents and lack of land due to the constraints of the South Downs National Park and the sea; the ever-widening gap between market rents and the level up to which housing benefit is paid; the local authority's lack of power and resources to properly manage the private rented sector; limitations on the council's own home-building scheme including constraints on lending, land and build costs versus long-term revenue expectations from affordable rents, and lack of sites big enough to see economies of scale; how far short of the city's five-year housing supply we are actually delivering; the impact of this on planning decisions and increasing ease with which those decisions can be reversed on appeal; exactly how short of meeting our housing need our City Plan is, and the direction laid down by the Planning Inspectorate to address that regarding the urban fringe; how sites in the fringe were assessed and chosen; the rigour of agreed policies on urban fringe development including sustainability, biodiversity net gain, public access and amenity, landscaping and heritage; and the limitations of a housing delivery structure offering rents significantly below market rates. It was because of the time I spent doing the job, time paid for by the taxpayer, so that I could make informed decisions on their behalf.

I don't care, a resident might still say: I still don't want it. But whether they care or not, those issues still exist. You said you wanted genuinely affordable housing for local people, I said to the Coldean campaigners: it was in the manifesto on which we got elected. We do, they said. We just don't want it here. Residents elsewhere in the city said the same about proposals in their area. But we can't deliver invisible housing. That would be impossible. It has to go somewhere.

The problem is that someone will often come along and claim that the impossible is possible. There's a widespread notion, for example, that public spending can be cut dramatically without it having any impact on public services. In reality, while there are always efficiencies to be made, chopping the budget of, let's say, a local authority, will inevitably have a negative impact on what that council can do for people. Pretending otherwise is simply misleading. There's a choice to be made. At the end of the day, if we want staffed libraries open decent hours, subsidised bus routes, more frequent street cleaning, youth services, and so on, there's a cost involved. We can collectively decide to pay for these services or not. But what many seem to expect – encouraged by politicians themselves and other opinion-formers – is both at the same time.

In terms of invisible housing, the local Conservatives opposed building on the urban fringe. They advocated pushing back on the Planning Inspectorate and adding loads more units on brownfield sites where high allocations were already being planned. Residents' groups in built-up areas didn't agree: they were campaigning for more units on the urban fringe, to avoid large-scale building in neighbourhoods that were already high-density. While the problem was pushed around the city, we were still nowhere near planning for our housing needs anyway: even if the density were upped everywhere we'd still have been short. Putting aside the delivery gap and defying the Planning Inspectorate wasn't, in my view, a position that the Conservatives could maintain if they took power.

I don't doubt that opposition groups of councillors up and down the country are doing similar things. Calling for something in opposition which you know isn't deliverable in power doesn't do anyone any favours at all and erodes trust in politicians even further. Extreme optimism, such as relying on the Planning Inspectorate to do a dramatic about-face when the fundamentals haven't changed, isn't a decent get-out. It would be more mature to fess up to the electorate when something they want isn't really an option whoever's in power – and that the housing has to go somewhere. It might help to stem those sky-high expectations. For sure, voters would need some time to get used to it. There'd still be huge pressure on politicians to find ways of agreeing with their residents whatever the circumstances, gamely dismissing the barriers and talking up the unfeasible. Then, when in power, guess what? It doesn't come off. And so we end up being hated – because we're trying too hard to be liked.

That's not to say that we can't address difficult problems. We absolutely can, but we'd have to be willing to pay, whether the cost is monetary or otherwise. We could have a better funded public sector with strong, effective interventions – but we should expect to pay higher taxes. We could have a smaller state with drastically reduced tax bills – but shoestring public services. All we need to do is choose. But we don't really go for one or the other. This is partly because some people want the former and some the latter, so we drift backwards and forwards somewhere in the middle. But it's also because we seem to be holding out for both. There are those – politicians among them – who seem intent on persuading the public that we can have top-notch services at rock-bottom prices, invisible housing, and numerous other impossible things. We should have the guts to be clear with voters about how things work and what they cost. But there will be plenty of times when this isn't what they want to hear.

We're Not All the Same

10. They Only Want to Line their Own Pockets

A resident gets in touch on Twitter. The shrubbery running alongside a pavement is overgrown again. Are you going to come out and take a look? they ask. Or are you just going to sit at home counting your allowance?

I might have taken offence at this but instead was amused at the image it generated of me sitting like Silas Marner in front of a hoard of gold coins, gleefully weighing each in my grubby little hand as I counted it into piles. An electronic payslip is nothing like as much fun. I ignored the jibe and got the bushes trimmed. My relationship with the resident improved. But for any politician who earns anything at all from their work (and even for some who don't), this kind of dig is pretty common.

A lot is said about politicians' pay, but it's rarely positive and never seems to be the whole story. Let's start by looking at the pay and responsibilities of 99.5% of politicians: councillors. They don't get a salary, and most councillors don't – and aren't expected to – do the job full time. Instead there's an allowance (tax-deductible), though many councils at the town and parish level opt not to have this either. The allowance is designed to make it easier for them to put some time aside for their duties. Someone who works full time might, with the allowance, be able to reduce their hours slightly so that they can get to daytime meetings and events. Those who take on special responsibilities, like leader of the council or committee chair, will get more. In the year from April 2016 to April 2017 (the first full calendar year of serving) I received an allowance of £14,085.48, consisting of

£11,879.64 basic allowance and an additional £2,205.84 for being Deputy Chair of the Housing Committee. These allowances are set by an independent committee, which takes into account that Brighton and Hove is a unitary council with responsibility for the whole gamut of local services. The amounts increased by a few percentage points each year and were revisited every election term by the committee. I didn't think the amounts were too shabby. The leader of the council in the same time period received £43,434.74 – nothing like a paid chief executive who would expect upwards of £150,000, but still a reasonable amount that enabled many elected council leaders to do the job full time.

It's not a fortune, though. Being a councillor isn't generally seen as a career and it certainly won't make anyone rich. For some, giving up their normal job to become a councillor would result firstly in a major income drop, and secondly in possible problems later on when wanting to take it up again. Being a councillor doesn't sit as well as one might think on a CV, because it's neither one thing nor another. It's not really a proper job, though it certainly feels like one sometimes. It can be tricky for someone with other commitments to find the time. The result is that council chambers up and down the country tend to be stocked with large numbers of retired people. Bless the retired and all they do for society: the rest of us would be lost without them. But the age range on many councils is often way out of alignment with the populations their members represent. That's a shame. The truth is, while there's a healthy rhetoric around politicians walking all over each other's backs in their single-minded pursuit of power, persuading people to stand as councillors is actually quite difficult. The allowance helps. If you don't have much of either time or money, sinking a load of hours into something that doesn't earn you anything just isn't feasible. Without it, the perspectives of many single parents, young people or anyone at the start of their career, or at the height of it, would be lost. But even so, it's difficult.

So what does the job actually involve? Before any talk of allowances, you have to get elected in the first place. In my experience, being a candidate in a marginal ward involved knocking on doors at least twice a week (some went out every day) and spending at least some time every day working on election literature, social media, going to meetings and events and generally getting involved in the local community. For this there's no pay at all, even for parliamentary candidates who sometimes need to put in a great deal more effort than this and give up work to campaign.

And if you're elected? I've kept all my diaries from that time. In the first few weeks after May 2015 I went to a number of ninety-minute or two-hour training sessions organised by the council, generally during office hours (they'd schedule them first thing in the morning or late afternoon to try and make it easier). Here are the sessions I attended:

- Planning (compulsory for anyone to sit on Planning Committee)

- Chairing skills
- Equalities
- The Code of Conduct
- Corporate parenting (our responsibilities towards children in care)
- CityClean (the bins, amongst other things)
- The Communications team
- Media training
- Adult Social Care
- Public Health
- Transport
- Children's Services
- Major projects (this involved a minibus tour of the city)
- The council's agricultural holdings (another minibus tour)
- The Communities team
- The Libraries team

Getting to, say, three or four of these a week for several weeks on the trot was pretty challenging for some of us. Many had understanding employers, or reduced their hours. Others took paid or unpaid leave. But it didn't stop there. Throughout the whole time I served, training sessions, briefings and workshops were scheduled constantly. These covered such key topics as homelessness, air quality, biodiversity and food poverty. I got the impression officers were disappointed that attendance at these events was often so low, with perhaps half a dozen councillors managing to get to something that all 54 of us had been invited to. I lost count of the number I would have liked to go to, but couldn't.

So much for induction and ongoing training. As for our actual role, the responsibilities of the new administration were divvied up at the first euphoric Labour Group meeting of councillors, when our delight at winning the election was tempered by our realisation that we were expected to run the council with just 23 members – we were the largest party by only a whisker. As well as each of us being on at least two committees (most of which met five times a year, but often with pre-meets and briefings, and always with hefty reports to read) there were Full Council meetings and all kinds of panels, boards and steering groups. Attempts had been made to cut down on these over the years, but it was very difficult to withdraw, and besides, a lot of the council's influence was through this kind of "soft" civic participation. For example, I served on the Music Trust, which had a pot of money to support music teaching in schools, and for a long while I chaired the city's Fair Trade steering group.

On top of this was the ward stuff: attending community meetings, showing up at events, holding surgeries and of course dealing with the queries of anyone who got in touch. There were some weekly chores, like remembering to look at the planning applications that had come in across the whole ward, and deciding whether to comment on any of them. Doorknocking is on top of this, but is the only way to reach the majority who don't participate in other ways. People had differing experiences with surgeries; mine usually granted me a pleasant hour of peace and quiet, interrupted only by a nice chat with the circuit training lady who had the hall after me. The trouble is, once you've advertised them you have to be there in case anyone shows up.

Councillors often got involved in additional things: I was a trustee of a charity that ran a community centre and supported local events, and I was also a school governor, something that could take up a lot of time in its own right, but many councillors did this on top. Party activities are essential for councillors representing a political party – which was almost all of us – but it's not considered part of the job as far as the allowance is concerned. These, for me, would include monthly constituency party meetings, monthly branch meetings (times two if you don't live in the same branch that you represent), member communications, campaign organisation, and showing up on invitation to speak about specific topics.

So what did this all add up to? I've just got out the 2018 diary and opened it randomly. In the week of November 12th, here's what I was doing.

Monday: At 9.30, a housing briefing meeting. 11.30 an internal Labour Group meeting. At 12.30, another one. At 1.30, Corporate Parenting Board, something I don't think I was formally on, but all councillors were invited in our capacity as corporate parents of children in care. At 3.30 I had a meeting with a senior officer. At 5.45 another internal group/party meeting. At 7 p.m. we had the weekly Group meeting, all councillors coming together. These lasted a couple of hours.

Tuesday: 10-12 some kind of training session. At 2.30 I had a private rented housing meeting, and another meeting of some sort in between the two.

Wednesday: Housing Committee, a meeting starting at 4 p.m. – but with a pre-meet an hour beforehand. They went on until they were finished, often as late as 9 p.m. Also that evening was the AGM of Hollingdean Residents Association. I would have had to send apologies, unless I managed to get there after the committee meeting.

Thursday: I have struck through that day, perhaps trying to ring-fence it for paid work. But in the evening it was "phoning". Probably a party phone bank.

Friday: another day struck through, but in the evening I was busy taking delivery of the Hollingdean News community newsletter and sorting it into bundles.

Saturday: Super Saturday! Generally a morning and afternoon of door-knocking.

Sunday: in the morning was a meeting of the executive of the Local Campaign Forum, a party body that oversees local election campaigns.

I can't remember if I actually went to all these things: I suspect not. I could manage more than some, but others did much more than me, often invisibly. In Belper, where I live now, if there's an event going on in town it's almost certain that several of the folk wandering about in high-viz vests are town councillors helping out on a voluntary basis.

In terms of unsung councillor work, I want to mention a particular example: fostering and adoption boards. These were the people – not just councillors – who made critical decisions about the lives of children and young people, and those who wanted to look after them. It was hard work – long reports of hundreds of pages detailing the history and situation of the child in question, followed by long meetings that had to agree important decisions about them. It wasn't work that anyone could publicly talk about, and it must have been pretty difficult at times. And yet these were often roles that people volunteered for, because it was so clearly so important. I sometimes think of the work of these boards up and down the country when faced with social media tropes about politicians who only care about money, only care about their own reputations.

My allowance, as I mentioned before, in the first full year was £14,085.48. I reckon when things were full-on I did about 30 hours a week. Things quietened down a lot during school holidays, though. Let's say I did 30 hours a week for 42 weeks of the year. That would mean I "earned" £11.17 per hour. A reasonable overall estimate would be £10-15 per hour, including community work that was really voluntary on top, and all the party stuff as well (and party rules also stipulate that Labour councillors donate a proportion of their allowance to Group funds). I was quite happy with this: £10-£15 an hour seems reasonable. It's not a fortune, though.

If I divide my 2016-2017 allowance by the number of voters in my ward, it comes to £1.21 each. Roughly speaking my residents each paid me just over £1 a year to represent them. In 2016-2017, the sum of all councillor allowances and expense claims (which were minimal, by the way) came to £843,969.10. There were 211,893 electors in Brighton and Hove in May 2015. That means that each voter paid roughly £3.98 each. Slightly more if you include allowances for the non-political mayor and deputy mayor. Most residents are represented by either two or three councillors, and the allowances of the leader and committee chairs were higher than mine. So overall, residents were getting the services of their local councillors for less than £5 a year. Sounds like a bargain to me!

These aren't the only costs of democracy. We were all supplied with IT equipment, there was a team of officers there to manage the councillors and the committee cycle, and on top of that the nature of public accountability and transparent decision-making impacted on all aspects of the council's work. Removing democracy from the council would, in the short term, probably save a great deal of time and money. In the longer term, however, without all that expensive accountability and transparency, I feel sure it would end up costing a lot more.

Of course £5 a year wouldn't be seen as a bargain by anyone who fundamentally disagrees with what their councillors are doing, or who thinks their councillors aren't doing anything. And sometimes that's the case. It's perfectly possible for someone to serve as a councillor for years and do practically nothing. There's no contract as such. Often, the only real requirement is attendance at Full Council meetings – but not necessarily even the whole meeting. Councillors' commitment to the role might wane for numerous reasons: falling ill, work or family commitments changing, or else the role just didn't suit, the inbox got too large, it wasn't what they expected, it all just got too nasty, and folk withdrew from the role but stayed in post. There should be a resignation and a by-election when this happens, but there wasn't always. Party whips would do what they could. Councils also have a complaints procedure, but in practice the council hardly has any sanctions to apply when a councillor is found to be lacking.

In theory the electorate will distinguish at the ballot box between those who are most or least effective or hardworking at the end of each term. The problem with that notion is firstly that it requires residents to have accurate knowledge about who their councillors are and what kind of job they've been doing, and secondly that there are multiple other ballot box issues that will trump a councillor's personal performance. Ask all the councillors up and down the country who lost their seats because of something their party did nationally that they may not even have agreed with. People I know well in the local community and worked alongside didn't vote for me because ideologically they preferred another party. I can't complain about this. I've asked myself if, at another time of life when I wasn't a Labour Party member, I'd vote locally for a Conservative if I thought they'd make an excellent councillor. No, is the answer. Their opinions and values on the bigger issues are just too different from my own, regardless of how committed an individual might be to the job itself. So the idea that the electorate will hold their representatives directly to account for the work they've been doing is somewhat flawed.

So, are councillors only in it for the money? I don't think so, because there isn't very much money involved, though some councillors are guilty of pocketing the allowance and not doing enough to justify it. Again, criticism where it's deserved is what democracy is all about: generalising about everybody only interferes with this.

What about the other 0.5% of politicians – MPs? It must be beyond doubt that the majority of the general public feel that MPs are overpaid and generally over-rewarded for what they do. I believe there are two different reasons for this. Firstly, they think MPs don't do anything, or at least nothing worthwhile. Therefore, every penny that's spent on them is a waste of money that could go to someone more deserving. Secondly, they think MPs are the ones who decide what other people get paid, and they selfishly use this power to enrich themselves while others struggle. The first of these is certainly not the case for everyone, though it's probably true of some. As for the second, MPs do have a role in setting public sector pay, and can legislate around pay and income for everyone else as well. But if the pay of an MP is too high if it's more than anyone else gets, that would mean paying MPs less than everyone else. In other words, minimum wage or some special salary that's below it. Or, indeed, nothing at all.

What's the problem? some people would say. It's all they deserve, isn't it? But to my mind there is a more important question to ask than what salary an MP deserves, and that is this: what salary level would best serve the interests of our democracy?

Unlike councillors, the job of an MP is full time. Much publicity ensues when MPs spend time on other things instead of their day job, and rightly so. But the MPs I've had dealings with, across different parties, all seem to work very hard. Ultimately, it's impossible to have a democracy without MPs. Do we want to attract good, talented people into the role? If so, we need an appropriate pay level. Not so high that people would only do it for the money, but not so low either that it will deter people who would do the job well. These are the kinds of questions that IPSA, the independent body which now sets MPs' pay, asks, along with considering what the job of an MP actually entails (and the role is getting bigger, according to them), what the pay is for similar types of role, and when it should go up over time. The conclusions they come to sometimes seem embarrassing to MPs, who quite rightly predict widespread resentment when MPs' pay goes up and others' do not, particularly with inflation and the cost of living on top of that.

Whether IPSA always gets it right is a matter for debate. My own view (as someone who earns a lot less than an MP) is that with the challenges we face, including low pay, social and economic exclusion and in-work poverty, we need good quality elected representatives, and that's worth paying for. The actual combined cost of MPs' pay and other expenses compared with the magnitude of the decisions they make is pretty small.

Trying to punish MPs by underpaying them would amount to shooting ourselves in the foot. We need to provide them with a suitable salary so that enough of them have the skills to do the job well. There are already entry barriers effectively preventing a lot of low-income people becoming MPs because no one gets paid for being a candidate, which can involve months or even years of campaigning on an all but full time basis, before you're elected in the first place.

All these arguments fall down in the face of the preconceived idea that there's no such thing as a good MP (or a good politician) and that they will all, without exception, be rubbish regardless of what they're paid. This sentiment interferes with any debate that might help to improve our democracy and the quality of MPs we get, and only leads us towards unworkable solutions. Which is a pity, because there definitely is scope for improvement and we should be striving to get there.

We've talked about pay, but it isn't just about pay. Politicians line their own pockets from the public purse, don't they? We know that from all the scandals over expenses, lobbying, failure to declare, and so on, that we hear so much about. The problem is that while it's essential that politicians are publicly held to account, we end up hearing only about the small number of people who may have broken the rules, and nothing at all about those who didn't. Once again the generalisations are widespread – two or three unpleasant revelations, and "they're all at it".

Tracey Hill

As a councillor, all I can remember claiming on expenses is two train fares to London to go to housing events. Most councillors claimed nothing at all (the details are all online)[xviii]. We had the use of a laptop, a phone and for a while a printer – for council business only – and could choose to get a bus pass that we contributed towards. We got fed every now and then, sometimes at long-running council meetings, but more often at outside events such as AGMs. I'm talking buffets: egg sandwiches and sausage rolls. And this backfired as a freeloading exercise if you showed up at an AGM for the buffet and ended up being treasurer for ten years.

There was also a budget for public involvement, which could be used for things like booking a room for a surgery and advertising it. Officers were pretty scrupulous in this area: they once refused to pay for a community hall I'd booked for a public meeting. Surgeries, yes: meetings, no (I paid for it myself).

Declarations are another area of great discussion. Basically, people can give you stuff but if they do, the public should know so that they can judge whether it might influence the decisions you make. That's why declaring things is so important. I had to declare anything that had been given to me in the course of being a councillor that was worth more than £50. Again, this was scrupulously administered. Amidst the great celebration when Brighton and Hove Albion made it into the Premier League, we all got given various bits of kit to wave around for the photos. I ended up with a scarf. This did not have to be declared. Anyone who was given a scarf

AND a shirt had to declare them. This was detailed to us all in a friendly email from the Democratic Services team.

Another time declarations mattered was at the annual Budget Council meeting, where councillors vote on an overall budget across all activities of the council. The declarations of interest at the start of this meeting went on for some time, as each of the 54 of us stood up to mention the charities where we served on the boards, the schools where we were governors, the jobs our spouses did – anything that might mean we were more than ordinarily affected by the budget. I don't know how aware the general public is of this process, but it was all taken pretty seriously. And so it should. The problem is that when some politician somewhere hasn't followed the rules, instead of drawing conclusions about that particular individual, perceptions of all politicians diminish.

What about corruption, then? The gravy train? People wanting favours? In the year I was chair of the Planning Committee I was forever nonplussed at the number of people I met who seemed quite happy, having known me no more than a few minutes, to suggest that I "knew all about the brown envelopes". I was advised to laugh it off, but the truth is that I never saw the funny side. Over time there have been bribery cases and corrupt individuals, but loads of professions and walks of life have seen appalling abuse without the entire caboodle being tarnished. If you met a doctor for the first time, would you playfully ask them how many patients they'd killed? Or a teacher whether they're in the habit of sleeping with their pupils? It seems a feature of politics that the very worst excesses are somehow assumed to reveal what's going on everywhere: instead of a bad apple, it's the tip of the iceberg.

The whole association of planning with bribery isn't helped by the fact that in every town and city up and down the country, there's at least one building which causes strangers to stop in the street, gaze up and say something like "How, in the name of all things holy, did *that* get planning permission?" I was frustrated at times myself when a decision just seemed perverse. But for the record, in my entire life, no one has ever offered me a bribe.

It seems to me that the more angry accusations of corruption came when either I had a view that someone didn't like, or they were frustrated that I couldn't do more to help them. One resident asked for my support with a planning application he was making. He wanted to do something which usually fell within permitted development (PD) and you don't need permission, but for some technical reason PD didn't apply. So he put in an application. It was refused. Why? The council said his proposal was boxy and unattractive. They all are round here, he pointed out, and he was right: the neighbourhood was full of similar builds done under PD. That's as may be, said the planning department. But we didn't get to decide on those. We do on yours, and it's boxy (I'm paraphrasing here). I sympathised with the guy and wrote in to support his appeal. But the appeal was unsuccessful. He sent me an angry letter about corruption in the planning department. I said I didn't think there was corruption though I didn't agree with the decision, but unfortunately there wasn't anything else I could do. "Then *you're* corrupt!" was his sign-off. We had no further correspondence.

While scandals and poor job performance are a reality, I don't think that people generally go into politics for the money. Several of my former colleagues have said that it took years for their finances to recover from their time as councillors. If I'd never bothered with politics and carried on working full time, I would undoubtedly be a lot richer now. I don't mind: I'm glad to have served and the allowances seemed reasonable. The only thing I did mind was when someone who barely knew me accused me of having my snout in the trough.

But this isn't just a minor irritation. Such assumptions drive a wedge between voters and the people who represent them, making it more difficult to consider important questions like how to make politics more representative of the population, and how to make our democracy and our government – at all levels – as good as it can possibly be. That is a massive missed opportunity.

11. They're Incompetent

I spoke at length to a couple on their doorstep. They were not happy. They'd lived in Brighton for several decades and had watched it, they said, decline. More people, more traffic, the parking was expensive, they were building everywhere. It used to be a nice town, neat and tidy with the verges cut regularly. But now – the students, the prices, the litter, the graffiti. They didn't even go to the city centre anymore. Brighton had been ruined.

I spoke to plenty of long-term residents who felt that their town had gone downhill. But what really struck me about this couple was that they attributed every single one of these changes entirely to the local council. The council allowed too many developments, encouraged people to move here, let all the students in, didn't keep the city clean, tolerated antisocial behaviour, charged WAY too much for parking ("We never go to the seafront any more") and so on. Without the interference of the council, they thought, Brighton would still be the same kind of place it was thirty or forty years ago.

We spoke so long that my door-knocking buddies had disappeared somewhere. But I couldn't generate even a glimmer of optimism. "Well, I'd better go," I said eventually, "before I decide to kill myself." Yes, I actually said that. I'm not proud: I was there to listen and should have managed to button it up. But their negativity defeated me.

The city vibe these residents weren't keen on was a bonus for many others: the buzz, the laissez-faire, the night life and so on. What this couple saw as a loss many more considered a gain. And was it all the doing of the council? The council didn't decide who could and couldn't come and live in the city. They couldn't dictate student numbers: the universities were free to expand as they wanted. In terms of developments, we were playing catch-up: many major developments had stalled in recent years. City centre parking charges came from a need to reduce massive congestion and poor air quality. Keeping the city clean – okay, we didn't have the best bin service in the country, and the city does have drug issues and other negative consequences of its night time economy. That was fair enough, perhaps. My point is that when things change, politicians aren't necessarily driving it.

In my experience the council was often responding to things that were changing for other reasons. The effectiveness of that response is definitely something citizens should have an opinion on. But is it really entirely the fault of politicians that the world isn't how we'd like it to be? I saw a guy on Facebook suggesting that politicians could end poverty tomorrow with the stroke of a pen. No wonder he's angry if that's what he thinks. If ever I had a chance to end poverty by signing my name somewhere, I'd have been more than keen (although I'd have wanted to take a good look at the small print). A corporate chief executive is held responsible for the performance of their company. They're not responsible for much beyond that. The job of a politician is far wider.

These high expectations of what the council could do led to some quite extraordinary demands at times. One hot summer, some folk became very concerned that the city's dewponds were drying out and the goldfish within were expiring in large number. Teams of volunteers were pictured in the press knee-deep in stinking mud scooping the gasping fish out and passing them to safety. Can't the council do something? they asked. They could top up the dewponds, couldn't they, in dry weather? It wouldn't be that big a deal to run a few hosepipes across the parks and downlands. Would it?

It was a while before the council responded to this. As an aside, some in the local press had a habit of asking the council for comment with a couple of hours' notice, generally expecting that in an organisation of maybe 8,000 employees, there must be someone who could provide a statement. The problem is that out of that entire staff, probably only two or three are fully equipped to give an authoritative answer as to why it might not be feasible to plumb in all the city's dewponds, and they may not be available at short notice. This is why you often see "The council was approached for comment" at the end of an article that presents only one side of an issue. Anyway, when it became available, the response ran along these lines: "Goldfish don't occur naturally in dewponds. Dewponds dry out in the summer. Please don't put goldfish in dewponds." And I know this is pretty rough on the goldfish, clearly the innocent victims in all of this.

I was asked one time to come to a residents' meeting for a block of flats. One of the residents, to the ire of the meeting organisers, had invited the local press along. It must have been a slow news week because they showed up. The guy who invited them had something of an agenda, or perhaps more than one. In the milling-about after the meeting, he took the journalist to one side and in a stage-whisper audible to the whole room, said "That Councillor Hill knows *nothing* about fire safety."

He wasn't wrong. Fire safety isn't my background at all. The horror of the 2017 Grenfell tragedy had a huge impact locally, with a massive focus on infrastructure, emergency procedures and inspections, and a big outreach exercise to council tenants and beyond. The councillors' role was to oversee what was being done, scrutinise the plans, check progress, and be there to respond to the concerns of residents. This particular resident had been in touch shortly after the tragedy with a long list of concerns about his block. I asked council officers and representatives from the fire service to speak with him directly: his points were pretty technical. They visited and spent a lot of time with him, but he remained unhappy. He wanted me to visit so that he could show me his concerns and persuade me to challenge the officers on what they had said. While I read everything he sent and spoke to him at length on the phone, I wouldn't take it any further. My approach was to go along with what the officers, and particularly the fire service, recommended (I spoke to both of them as well). If the fire service thought it was safe, I was happy. After all, they're the people who have to go in if there were a fire. And they had years of experience and actual knowledge. I didn't.

In plenty of other spheres of activity, some are called upon to supervise or take responsibility for the work of others who know more than them. An IT project manager, for example, will have programmers, analysts and coders in their team with specialist knowledge of the software and programming languages that they work with. The project manager relies on them, and can't step in and do the work for them. But it's still the project manager ultimately responsible for the successful completion of the project. Trustees of charities and other volunteers such as school governors also have a scrutiny role over the paid executives who are actually running things and will generally know much more about it. In these cases, distinctions are drawn between strategic direction and operational matters. The trustees and the governors have a role in high-level decisions about where the organisation is going, but it's the staff that make it happen. In politics, however, these lines seem blurred as politicians tend to be held responsible – in the court of public opinion, anyway – for operational misadventures as well as strategic mistakes.

Locally some opposition councillors had a tendency to try and carve out a bigger and bigger role in relation to paid officers: calling for councillors to sit on every working group; referring projects back to committee repeatedly even once the strategic direction had been set; describing every internal meeting that wasn't public as "secret", and suggesting that it was lax to leave officers to do the job they'd been delegated to do. To my mind this confuses roles and suggests that the elected should be carrying out roles best done by people who are qualified to do it.

Councillors, and other elected politicians, are generalists. They have no expertise, or if they do, it's by-the-by and isn't the reason they're in post. Not that it can't be useful. One of our group used to be a paint salesman. Whatever was being discussed, he could be relied upon to speak eloquently on any paint-related issues that might arise, of which there was a surprising number. With my market research background, I could have spent my time critically appraising all consultations on the hunt for sample bias or leading questions (and I saw a few). But I didn't. I focused on doing what I'd been elected to do – give ordinary folk a place at the table and a role in ultimately determining what's important and what isn't. It was for others to look after the detail, though to be honest it never felt that way.

The fear that most often kept me awake at night was that something terrible would happen and people would demand to know why I hadn't anticipated it or asked about it. I asked about everything I could think of, but I still relied on people who knew a lot more than me. I could have spent all of our limited meeting time requesting risk assessments and contingency plans for every worst possible scenario, but that would have meant losing sight of what we were there to do, like a pedestrian so busy watching their feet to avoid tripping over that they walk in front of a bus.

And you know that idea that it's okay to say if you don't know something? There's a certain delight amongst commentators when revealing the ignorance of a politician. A colleague admitted that he had no idea how many visitors were coming to Brighton and Hove. Given that he was the lead member for tourism and the economy, this might seem something of an omission. The local newspaper certainly thought it was. But he'd been fully briefed, and was making the point that the data we had on visitors was patchy to say the least. For example, it only included people who'd visited the city by coach, which seems completely inadequate for starters. So getting an accurate idea of how we were doing as a tourism destination was very difficult for everyone, not just him. This subtlety, let's just say, didn't carry through into the press. What we learn from this is that it's better to flannel around than to admit there's something you don't know. Is the electorate best served in this way?

Of course politicians should be able to demonstrate sufficient knowledge to do their job. The situation is different for government ministers who are doing the job full time and in some cases are responsible for running a department. But they're still generalists, and are always advised by others with more expertise than them. The job of the elected is to make decisions based on the information they're given. Clearly, some make much better decisions than others, for example by deciding to listen to the expert advice as opposed to ignoring it. They should be held to account for these decisions, but I'm not convinced that the distinction between the political role and the role of officers who carry out their decisions is well understood, or penetrates some of the simplistic and relentlessly negative political commentary

The requirements to stand for election at any level are pretty minimal. This is deliberate. We want to enable people with all kinds of backgrounds to serve, so that we're represented by people who resemble the population at large as closely as possible. Stringent criteria in terms of skills and experience would run counter to this. Are our expectations from the people we elect in line with the way in which we choose them?

There is, however, nothing wrong with high expectations in general. Citizens should absolutely expect things to get better as a result of the actions of their politicians. Despite the crises and chaos of recent months, we should still have every confidence that our democratic system can deliver great things. We know it can – because it already has.

We're Not All the Same

Tracey Hill

12. Nothing Ever Changes

We're Not All the Same

"They don't make any difference," a woman was saying to my door-knocking chum and me as we enquired as to her general political loyalties. "Nothing ever changes. Labour, Conservative, it's all the same. People still struggle. They get no help."

Not so, we argued, and pointed to a number of things delivered by the last Labour government, such as tax credits and the strengthening of the state pension.

"You really think that?" she asked. "That they actually helped people?"

"Yes!" we chimed in unison with wide-eyed enthusiasm. She looked at us as though we were a pair of moon-crazed numpties.

Her statement was so sweeping, and yet it wasn't unusual. Why is it so difficult for people to believe that politicians have achieved anything? Perhaps because the best work of politicians is long term. There's that image of a swan gliding along, all that paddling invisible under the water. To me politics feels like that, only upside down. We see all the desperate paddling but lose sight of where we're heading. Most of the work of politicians can only be appreciated if you take a step back, and how often do we do that? The news is about what's changed since yesterday, not over the past ten years, or twenty. Yet it's these longer term changes that are the more profound.

Off the top of my head, here are ten big-picture things that have got better in my lifetime, at least partly due to the work of politicians. I could easily think of another ten, but these came to mind first.

Drink driving

When I was growing up, drinking and driving was commonplace. Now it's highly unusual. It's not even about staying below the limit: the norm now is not to drink at all if you're driving. Like everything in this list, this has been a joint achievement, key elements of which are the legislation and, probably more importantly, the communication, all those terrifying ads year after year. People are alive today who wouldn't be if it weren't for this sustained effort which succeeded in changing social norms.

Cleaner beaches

Our beaches are much more pleasant places to spend time, our bathing waters cleaner. In 1991[xix], only around 75% of coastal bathing waters were of sufficient quality for bathing. In 2017 it was 96% and these days it's close to 100%. This trend goes back to 1976, the year of the first European Bathing Water Directive, but it's hard to track down stats that go back that far. In fact, the first Google searches come back with press-release-driven stories about the latest beach cleans and how much litter there is compared with two or three years ago, or even just last year – a good example of how long-term changes often go unacknowledged.

LGBT rights

I grew up in a homophobic world. It's now much easier for a whole load of people to live openly without fear or prejudice. Labour reversed Section 28 and moved us forward with equalising the age of consent, adoption rights and civil partnerships, while Cameron's Conservative government brought in gay marriage. Of course there are still issues, but as ever we dwell on those and often overlook how far we've come.

Health and safety

Here we go, the oft-derided "Elf and safety" – but seriously, no one should be dying at work or suffering life-changing injury in entirely preventable accidents. When I was a kid, we used to wander around freely on building sites. The refuse collectors would heft open-topped metal bins onto their shoulders to carry them down rickety garden steps. Politics and legislation are a big part of these improvements, alongside the work of trade unions, which, by the way, doesn't usually generate much media interest unless there's a strike in the offing.

Recycling

Back in the eighties, if you were keen you could drive your empties to a bottle bank and pass a few fun minutes chucking them in the holes and hearing them smash. That was about it. Now you can recycle pretty much anything.

What isn't part of the doorstep collection can generally be taken elsewhere. Now that soft plastics (plastic bags etc.) are collected at the supermarket, the only things that get thrown into my bin are occasional food waste that can't be composted and the odd bit of packaging made from composite material. In Brighton and Hove, before I even started on the council, almost nothing was going into landfill: what couldn't be recycled went to an incineration plant that produced energy for the grid.

Better city centres

I grew up near Birmingham, with its Bull Ring shopping centre, Rotunda and Digbeth Road Coach Station, surely a contender for the worst place in the world to wait for a bus. Birmingham now is transformed, with its International Convention Centre, regenerated Gas Street canal basin, huge funky library and many other things including a completely rebuilt coach station. Most cities have gone through a similar improvement and are a whole load nicer than they were in the seventies and eighties. And, due to the general drop in crime rates that started in the mid nineties, safer.

The internet

Okay, politicians didn't invent the internet. But politicians ultimately enable and regulate our access to it. Remember dial-up? Superfast "always-on" broadband was a dream back in the nineties. And thanks to politicians we have consumer rights legislation to protect us from providers who don't give us what we pay for. Imagine COVID-19 without the internet. It made such a difference. Not everyone is online, of course. The UN has an ambition to extend internet access more universally across the globe. In the meantime the authoritarian governments of China and North Korea, for example, systematically limit or block access entirely, while some countries by contrast consider access to the internet a civil or human right.[xx]

AIDS

AIDS scared the hell out of me, particularly the chilling *Don't Die of Ignorance* 1987 advertising campaign. But while overtly fearmongering, it was also successful[xxi]: HIV-positive rates didn't go anywhere near as high as some predicted. Norman Fowler, the minister overseeing this campaign, has been working ever since on AIDS and HIV issues and LGBT rights, recently giving up his role in the House of Lords to focus on it. Previously a killer, an HIV-positive diagnosis these days doesn't have to impact on life expectancy as long as it's treated. Locally, Brighton and Hove became a Fast Track City in 2016 working towards the 90:90:90 targets driving HIV-positive awareness and treatment. This target has now been exceeded, not just in Brighton and Hove but across the UK.[xxii]

Domestic abuse

Decades ago, if you ended up with a husband who was a "wife-beater", you were just unlucky. You were expected to put up with it as best you could. Over a long period of time things have changed. Legislation now recognises patterns of coercive control that go wider than single acts of violence[xxiii], and domestic abuse is now an area of focus within the police. Among the many campaigners on this issue, Hove MP Peter Kyle has pushed for better processes for dealing with abusers in the family courts[xxiv]. Yes, there are mistakes, and their horrific consequences get the airplay they deserve. Sadly, domestic abuse is still a reality for far too many – but again, that's no reason to forget how far we've come.

Smoking

When I caught the bus to school, you could smoke on the top deck. When I was old enough to go into pubs, you could smoke in there as well. In 1974, 45% of British adults over 16 smoked; in 2020 it was 14%[xxv]. Plenty of folk didn't like the smoking ban of 2006-2007. They said it would close pubs, and maybe it did. But it also saved lives, as does all of the legislation around smoking including the constraints on advertising and the taxation that makes it so expensive.[xxvi]

Reading through this list, I'm struck by how many of them relate to one thing, the thing we value more than anything: life itself. Increased life expectancy is rarely discussed and it won't often be headline news. But it's real, and it's significant. In the early 1960s, UK life expectancy was around 71. In the years up to 2020 it was around 81[xxvii]. This is partly a triumph of modern medicine, but only in part, as the list above shows. Advances in medical knowledge mean nothing unless they're implemented, and for that you need politicians, to oversee either direct provision of healthcare or its regulation. Outside of that sit campaigns and communications aimed to change public behaviour and make our environments safer. Nothing is exclusively delivered by politicians, and maybe that's part of the problem – it's not straightforward to say who made something happen when lots of people did – but politicians were in there somewhere, their decisions and priorities influencing the direction of travel. The result? More Christmases, more summers, more chances to see grandchildren growing up. More of everything. More than a barrel of mud, anyway.

We live longer, more healthy lives. We're also better off. Average disposable incomes in 2020-21 were well over double what they were in 1977, even taking inflation into account[xxviii]. Our lives are in many ways more comfortable than they were fifty years ago. This isn't to belittle the hardship caused by inflation and soaring living costs that will impact deeply on individuals, families and communities for years. I'm talking about the gradual, often unnoticed, decades-long trends which have made life in the 2020s so different from how it was in the 1970s. And yes, people earn money through work and their own economic efforts, but government has a massive influence on their abilities to do so (providing education and training and regulating employment) and their freedom to enjoy what they earn (taxing at a reasonable but non punitive level, providing a reliable legislative framework in which to do business, influencing costs, pricing and consumer rights, and delivering key services including some form of welfare state). The years have seen plenty of jolts and backward steps, but if all politicians really were as terrible as so often described, would our world really look like this? Taken as a whole, is our experience of life appalling enough to justify these damning generalisations?

What about locally? For the really significant changes we'd need to look at those areas on which all the parties generally agreed, the underwater bulk of the Iceberg of Agreement, which could be addressed over a period of time longer than any individual administration. Major developments would be one: a team was put in place to work in whatever partnerships were necessary to get big developments off the ground, and some positive results were seen in our time. I'd also single out events: most summer weekends saw something going on in the city, often on the seafront. The visitor economy is definitely one of the city's successes, even if it's difficult to quantify sometimes. While not everyone shared this definition of success, the fact that so many people have visited the place underpins its popularity, which in turn makes it attractive for residents, young people, businesses, developers, event organisers, investors of all kinds, and yet more visitors.

In my specific field, HMO (houses of multiple occupancy) regulation strengthened during our time, together with planning limits on the number of conversions and, critically, a surge in purpose-built student accommodation, dramatically reducing demand for HMO conversions, which were eating into the stock of family homes. "It'll never happen," an HMO developer confidently said to me about the city's long-term purpose-built student housing plans. Well – it did.

There are a multitude of other ways in which the city of Brighton and Hove benefitted from the work, leadership and decisions of councillors (alongside many others). This is true of cities, boroughs, districts, parishes, towns and counties up and down the country. We don't talk about these things often enough outside of the realm of electioneering, where unfortunately much of it is dismissed as spin. In this way we risk entirely missing the biggest benefits democracy has brought us.

To put against this, some things haven't improved as much as they should have. Equality is one: while average life expectancy and living standards have improved, this hasn't been evenly distributed and the gap has increased. Is this because a self-interested political elite is failing to deliver something that people are clamouring for? I'm not so sure. I think many people tend to see interventions to promote equality as a threat, that they might lose out. "But what about equality for *me*?" one woman protested once, in response to my attempt to explain a proposal for secondary school catchment areas.

Another consistent failure is climate change. We've known about our impact on the planet for decades. We already have technologies which could dramatically reduce our emissions. A whole host of low-carbon alternatives are at our fingertips, but we persist with an unsustainable way of life. Is this because politicians across the board, for their own reasons, refuse to take the necessary steps? Or is it that while many people do, in theory, want us to address climate change, they'd prefer it to happen in a way which didn't impact on them very much? Perhaps politicians could disappear off somewhere and tinker around backstage – pull a few levers, swap over a few wires – and we can all just carry on as we are but on a low-carbon footing. This would be convenient, but not necessarily realistic.

A common narrative is that society is not the way it should be because of the unwillingness or incapacity of politicians to deliver what people want. But what if politicians *are* delivering what people want? That would change everything. On the minus side, we as citizens would have to take responsibility for how things are. It isn't them, as it turns out: it's us. On the plus side, the idea that we can't determine our collective fate is false. We can, if our vision is achievable and if enough people share it.

We're Not All the Same

13. So What?

We're Not All the Same

In a key 1975 episode of *Doctor Who*, Tom Baker stands staring at two bare wires, one in each hand. If he puts them together he will destroy the Daleks. It will be exactly as if they never existed and all the evil and suffering they inflicted will not have happened. But he hesitates. What about the civilisations that the Daleks brought together, united by a common enemy? Didn't good come out of their existence as well as bad? Does he have the right?

Does it really matter if people whinge a bit about politicians? Life is hard, after all, and politicians are powerful and should expect their actions to foster resentment. As we saw in the parking meeting, even those with opposing views can bond over the general belief that politicians are to blame for the state of things. Perhaps our seething resentment of those who represent us is actually a kind of social glue that stops us from going hammer and tongs at each other.

If you can't stand the heat, I've been told more than once, get out of the kitchen. That would be easy enough. I can think of any number of friends and colleagues who backed away from politics because of the sheer unpleasantness of it all, or declined to step up in the first place. But what then? Who would be left in the kitchen? A select group of those who are immune to the heat, while those with more sensitivity have gone away and left them to it? We would end up being led by those with the skin of rhinoceri, distinctive by their ability to shake off whatever is thrown at them.

I don't want to grow a thick skin. I don't want to habitually brush it off whenever someone insults me. I still want to listen, to get where people are coming from, to consider and reconsider, to care enough about criticism to be hurt by it sometimes. I want to remain fully human. If you prick me, I want to bleed. But at times in the job I felt caught in the centre of a pack of barking dogs, pulled and pushed by competing points of view, detested by all. The vehemence coming from voters some of the time is almost palpable, their disappointment and loathing, their cynicism at the prospect that anything can get better, that anything can actually work. The positives are out there but overlooked, the instances of our collective direction being shaped by public opinion trampled in the rhetoric. It's easier in some ways to think that we, the public, have no responsibility for the way things are. But what if we do? We'd have to look to ourselves to try and make things right – or else persuade others of our view of what right consists of. We'd have to be sure that we really want it, because there are no miracles out there and whatever it is will probably come at a price.

This is how democracy is supposed to work. You can't please everyone, so we have votes and decide things by the will of the majority. In my experience on the job, we were doing just that. Could we have performed better to deliver in the public interest? I'm sure we could, but we did okay. It certainly wasn't terrible. It was a mixed bag. But then most things are, aren't they? We accept the less than perfect in other aspects of life. So why do we expect so much more from politics? It's partly due to the political commentary that always focuses on those aspects of every initiative that didn't go so well, leaving the impression that with a bit more commitment or competence perfection could have been achieved. Politicians themselves are guilty of talking up expectations, especially in opposition, and should deal more in realism, though that would require an electorate prepared to hear the message.

Underneath all the talk, what I see is democracy working more or less as it should, but it's not recognised as such. For as long as it's not valued, there's a danger that something else could come along that looks better. Something a bit shinier, or someone with more pizzazz and personality, with a little more promise, just might steal the limelight. If electing people doesn't work, maybe something else will, right?

Spoiler: Doctor Who does go on to destroy the Daleks. But there the comparison ends, because if politicians were no more, what would we have instead? I sometimes ask this on the doorstep, but haven't yet heard a concrete answer. I've often suggested to the universal critics that they could stand themselves and give it a go. No success as yet. This is frustrating, as I know that just a day in office could shift their perspectives dramatically.

We talk a lot about low levels of trust in politicians. But in a sense, trust is the wrong word. The whole point about public accountability and transparency is that you don't need to trust your politicians. You can follow everything they do and evaluate their performance directly. You can get rid of them if you want. Instead of asking people if they trust politicians, perhaps it would be more in line with the nature of democracy to ask them how much they know about what their politicians are doing for them. How involved are they? Or, if they say they don't trust their politicians, ask them what they're doing about it. If a politician challenged voters in this way it probably wouldn't win them a lot of votes, but democracy is meant to be an active process in which we're all invested. If you don't like it, you have the power and the right to do something about it. And if you've already stepped up and still don't like it, persuade enough people to come with you and try to change things. If you still think everyone is rubbish after that, at least you've earned the right to feel that way.

I'm enough of a realist to know that this argument will be rejected by many, who have been led to believe that it's exclusively politicians who should be the agents of change. What can we do to engage people more in the political system? Education, some say. Well, it wouldn't do any harm and it's always heartening to meet young people enthusiastic about politics. What about such things as citizens' assemblies, which try and interest folk in the arguments and involve them more deeply in the decision-making process? Sounds good, but they only involve a handful of people. We had one in Brighton and Hove in relation to tackling climate change, and it doesn't seem to have resulted in an outbreak of peace around the difficult topics such as cycle lanes. More elections? I'm uneasy about this given the tiny turnouts for non-events like the police and crime commissioner elections. More referenda? But that leaves us open to the problem of distilling a complicated decision down into a yes/no question, and then trying to figure out after the event what it was that people actually wanted. We all know about that.

My best left-field suggestion for greater local inclusion is to replace councillors with something like jury service. Residents get called up randomly to take their turn, and for six months they make all the key decisions, taking advice from officers in the same way that a jury takes guidance from a judge. Completely unworkable? Probably, but I'd enjoy seeing Mr Angry trying to chair that parking meeting.

Here's an idea that's a lot easier: for one day a year all politicians agree to put their differences aside and speak only about what we have in common. The PM would be expected to stand and pay tribute to the Leader of the Opposition – and vice versa. All other speakers would follow suit, and the same in council chambers across the country. This would – if it made the news – remind us all that while debate and criticism are essential, all of it happens within a system which grants us the freedom to do it and which over time has brought huge benefits to our lives. Perhaps this could happen on the anniversary of the day Jo Cox was murdered. Or the day David Amess was murdered. Or the day Putin invaded Ukraine. Or the day a mob stormed the US Capitol. Or the day thousands of protesters were killed by their own government in Tiananmen Square in 1989. Or the day of the first of Stalin's Great Purges in 1936. Or the day of Hitler's Enabling Act in 1933. History isn't short of reminders of what democracy has given us, and how much we have to lose.

It's Remembrance Sunday at the war memorial close to Brighton's Palace Pier. We're lined up, all the civic dignitaries, watching the wreaths being laid, some of us laying one or two. At eleven o'clock the cannon is fired. Every seagull in the city takes to the wing and circles above. Their cries are only just dying down at the end of the two minutes' silence. The Last Post. Poems, prayers, then the parade resumes. They come back down past the viewing platform and every head in the formation turns sharply to the right, eyes on us, as they march past.

This "Eyes Right" is a visual show of respect for the leaders, those in authority. We have organised society so that those at the top are put there through the will of the people, to guide and lead according to the people's wishes. At moments like that I was incredibly proud to be a part of it, up there on that platform. I'm still proud, but also bruised, because so many seem so jaded by it all.

Democracy ought to be a way of getting people to buy in to the decisions made on their behalf, and yet somehow it doesn't. It should empower us to influence change so that we move forward in the way we want, yet so many feel defeated and ignored and can't see that they've played a role. In my experience the range of options, the possible actions, the choices we could make seemed so constrained, and at the same time the expectation could almost be limitless. And yet I'm still involved because despite all the noise, it does work, after a fashion: almost imperceptibly we drift towards something better, whenever there's enough common ground to agree what better is.

I said I didn't have a masterplan and I don't. But I would like to see those engaged in political debate – and that's a lot of people in addition to politicians and journalists – do more to distinguish between criticism of a person, a party or an idea and outright dismissal of politics as a whole. If we value democracy, let's defend it. That means not just being swept along on a wave of general cynicism but calling it out, overtly drawing attention to the instances where holding specific people responsible for something turns into an attack on the entire system. Any blanket dismissal of "all politicians" is a statement of failure: it's the same as saying that democracy isn't worth having.

If after reading this, the "all" is more often "some", I would consider that a win of sorts. If, when I'm next door-knocking, a few more voters decide not to make their minds up about me before I've figured out how to open their garden gate, that would be a step forward. If the next door we knock on is yours, please don't slam it. Give us a minute or two, the benefit of the doubt, even. You might find some of us are not that bad.

Comments and Feedback

If you have anything to say in response to the points in this book, there is a Facebook page (search for We're Not All the Same). I also intend to post there on current events and how they relate to the content of this book.

If you'd like to go onto my mailing list for updates or future publications, please visit my website, traceyhillauthor.co.uk. I am also on Facebook at facebook.com/traceyhillprofile and Twitter at @TraceyMHill.

Acknowledgements

For years I've been banging on to fellow Labour campaigners and others that I was going to write a book about why people hate politicians so much. I suspect this isn't the book a lot of them thought I'd be writing. But it's the one that I think needs writing, and despite the apparent efforts of those currently in government to turn everyone against politics forever, I still think it needs to be said. So thank you to everyone who endured my rants over the years: I appreciate it.

A number of people I have campaigned and worked alongside read early drafts and provided feedback. It has proven impossible to act on all the helpful suggestions they made, but I've no doubt this is a better book as a result of their time and input: Simon Burgess, Emma Daniel, David Lepper, Gill Mitchell, Warren Morgan, Caroline Penn, and Dan Wilson.

Tatiana Wilde at Reedsy provided me with an industry opinion along with many useful suggestions for improvement. Jackie Weaver took the time to read and comment on many parts of the text, and I've incorporated several updates and corrections as a result.

Matthew Flinders, author of the 2012 book *Defending Politics: Why Democracy Matters in the 21st Century*, has been influential in linking my thoughts and experiences into a broader narrative. Its central argument was described as unfashionable and it probably remains so, but it's also, to my mind, correct.

Jeanne Lolness patiently produced the cover art and cartoons after multiple iterations which I very much enjoyed, while Ryan O'Hara designed the cover.

I am an independent author: all errors are mine alone, and if you contact me with details I will endeavour to correct them.

About the Author

Tracey Hill is a history graduate from the University of Oxford and has earned a living teaching English in Budapest and Tokyo. A market researcher by profession, she is now an editor and writer on subjects involving people, place and politics. She has published a series of international spy thrillers under the pen name T.M. Parris. This is her first non fiction book.

She joined the Labour Party in 2008 and became an active campaigner and voluntary organiser. She first stood for election as a council candidate in 2011 and was elected in 2015, when Labour also became the largest party on Brighton and Hove City Council. During that administration she was Deputy Chair of the Housing and New Homes Committee with particular responsibility for private rented housing. In 2019 she was re-elected and became Chair of the Planning Committee. Labour remained the largest party at that election but the Green Party took control in the summer of 2020. In February 2021 she moved to Belper, Derbyshire, for family reasons and resigned her seat. She is still involved in campaigning in her local area.

Endnotes

[i] https://www.ukonward.com/reports/the-kids-arent-alright-democracy/
[ii] https://fullfact.org/online/false-claims-about-mps/
[iii] https://www.youtube.com/watch?v=BEqs7acA_50
[iv] https://labour-renaissance.org.uk/renaissance-report-labour-former-voters/
[v] https://en.wikipedia.org/wiki/The_West_Wing#Realism
[vi] https://lgiu.org/local-government-facts-and-figures-england/#section-4
[vii] https://www.carnegieuktrust.org.uk/publications/gdwe-a-spotlight-on-democratic-wellbeing/
[viii] https://www.local.gov.uk/our-support/leadership-workforce-and-communications/comms-hub-communications-support/futurecomms-1
[ix] https://www.brighton-hove.gov.uk/health-and-wellbeing/about-public-health/brighton-hove-joint-health-and-wellbeing-strategy-2019
[x] https://democracy.brighton-hove.gov.uk/ieListMeetings.aspx?CId=884&Year=-1
[xi] https://www.youtube.com/watch?v=cNOvQQQnAV8
[xii] https://commonslibrary.parliament.uk/research-briefings/cbp-8060/
[xiii] https://www.statisticsauthority.gov.uk/
[xiv] https://www.bbc.co.uk/news/uk-60250678
[xv] https://www.theargus.co.uk/news/11159115.parking-restrictions-in-lewes-road-triangle-will-damage-trade/
[xvi] https://democracy.brighton-hove.gov.uk/mgIssueHistoryHome.aspx?IId=41062&Opt=0
[xvii] https://en.wikipedia.org/wiki/Harold_Macmillan#1959_general_election
[xviii] https://www.brighton-hove.gov.uk/council-and-democracy/councillors-and-committees/councillors-allowances

We're Not All the Same

[xix] https://www.eea.europa.eu/themes/water/europes-seas-and-coasts/assessments/state-of-bathing-water/country-reports-2017-bathing-season/united-kingdom-2017-bathing-water-report

[xx] https://en.wikipedia.org/wiki/Right_to_Internet_access

[xxi] https://www.bbc.co.uk/news/magazine-15886670

[xxii] https://themartinfisherfoundation.org/brighton-hove-gets-fast-track-city-status/

[xxiii] https://www.womensaid.org.uk/information-support/what-is-domestic-abuse/coercive-control/

[xxiv] https://www.peterkyle.co.uk/uncategorised/2018/09/13/domestic-violence-in-family-courts/

[xxv] https://www.ons.gov.uk/peoplepopulationandcommunity/healthandsocialcare/drugusealcoholandsmoking/bulletins/smokingprevalenceintheukandtheimpactofdatacollectionchanges/2020#:~:text=The%20proportion%20of%20adults%20aged,2019%20was%20not%20statistically%20significant.

[xxvi] https://www.independent.co.uk/life-style/health-and-families/health-news/smoking-ban-has-saved-40-000-lives-856885.html

[xxvii] https://commons.wikimedia.org/wiki/File:Life_expectancy_in_the_largest_European_countries.png

[xxviii] https://www.ons.gov.uk/peoplepopulationandcommunity/personalandhouseholdfinances/incomeandwealth/bulletins/householddisposableincomeandinequality/financialyearending2021

Printed in Great Britain
by Amazon